This study by Ed Horak will help Christians understand spiritual warfare and practically engage victoriously in it. In past years, Ed has put out a number of outstanding books to equip and engage the faith of believers. In "Authority in the Spirit Realm," Ed has done another masterful job of mining a strategic biblical topic. He has picked up this area so critical to the successful walk of every believer and examined it like a gemstone. He has then helped to cut and polish that stone in a way that makes each facet shine and clearly reflect light and truth from God's Word back to the reader. A great read!

Dr Berin Gilfillan
(Missionary, CEO – International School
Of Ministry, San Bernardino, CA)

"Authority in the Spirit Realm" is a much needed book on victorious Christian living. Too many Christians have been taught a distorted gospel, and fail to realize their position in Christ and the authority they possess as the sons and daughters of God! Pastor Ed Horak has outlined these truths in a powerful, yet applicable way that is sure to take any believer into the higher life Christ died to bring us. Ed shows the believer how to enforce Christ's victory over every area of their lives! This is essential reading for any Christian desiring to go to the next level in their walk with the LORD!

Jurgen Matthesius
(International Conference Speaker and
Senior Pastor C3 Church, San Diego, CA)

Ed Horak latest book "Authority in the Spirit Realm" is a theologically sound must read for every Christian who wishes to grow in the knowledge of the Lord Jesus Christ. It is theologically sound and if you sincerely desire to walk in the fullness of the grace provided by Jesus then the information laid out in these few pages will bring you to that point. The authority God has given us as believers, has been presented by Rev Horak in a concise and accurate teaching free from denominational interpretation. His wealth of knowledge gained from years as Dean of various Bible Colleges is evident, but his grasp of this truth is the most impressive aspect of this book.

Henry Wolmarans M.Th, D.Min, PhD
(Author of "Your Rights to Riches" and "Yes You Can Achieve Your Dreams" and Senior Pastor: The Promise Church, San Diego, CA).

Authority In The Spirit Realm

Ed Horak

Contents

Jesus lived and died for us, and is now alive forevermore with all authority. God's government is on the increase!

Chapter 1

Who Is Winning The Fight?

In a ten round boxing match you can lose every one of nine rounds on points, but if you score a knockout in round ten, you win the fight. Of course, there is no fun in getting beaten up in any round on the way to victory, but in the end you still win the fight! Right now, you may be in a battle in some area of your life. Perhaps you have a sickness, or financial difficulties, maybe even some family troubles. Things look bleak. When you turn on TV, the world looks like it is going down the tubes itself. There appears to be little hope, great despair, crazy fuel prices, disease, famine, and disaster. You sit back in a numbed state, and wonder what is really going on, and also what the future will hold?

A fair question might be, 'Who is actually winning the fight, spiritually speaking'? Right now, it looks like satan and his evil cohorts are doing a pretty good job of messing things up on planet earth. The war for the souls of men is raging as intensely as it ever was, and you and I are in the middle of a world seemingly gone mad. Preachers say God is in control, but to you, it may not look like it right now! In fact it often looks as if unseen forces are at play, and they are outside your control.

I believe as you read on you will discover a helpful perspective that will encourage you to take your proper place of authority in God's kingdom. There is a place of fruitfulness and fulfillment reserved just for you that no adversary can or should hold back.

Things are not always the way they seem at first. From your point of view, they seem one way, but when seen from God's viewpoint, everything changes. He is all knowing, and sees the big picture, whereas you and I only know and matter in part. We do not know everything at any one moment like God. Fortunately, God has given us His Word which communicates absolute and eternal truth: the way things truly are. Authority can only be understood and exercised from this viewpoint. This book looks into the higher reality of authority in the unseen realm of the spirit, and how you can play your part in exercising the authority God has given you to in Christ.

When It Looks Like One Thing...

When it looks like satan's power over the affairs of mankind is growing, God's word says that there will be no end to the increase of His government! Jesus was born, and is now alive forevermore with all authority, and God's government is on the increase!

Isaiah 9:6-7
For unto us a Child is born,
Unto us a Son is given;
And the government will be upon His shoulder.
And His name will be called
Wonderful, Counselor, Mighty God,
Everlasting Father, Prince of Peace.
Of the increase of His government and peace
There will be no end,
Upon the throne of David and over His kingdom,
To order it and establish it with judgment and justice
From that time forward, even forever.
The zeal of the LORD of hosts will perform this.

Do you know someone who is stubbornly refusing to bow his or her knee in worship to God? The Word of God says that every knee will eventually bow. Maybe not in this immediate time on earth, but in the sweep of eternity, every knee will bow.

Philippians 2:9-11
Therefore God also has highly exalted Him and given Him the name which is above every name, that

at the name of Jesus every knee should bow, of those in heaven, and of those on earth, and of those under the earth, and that every tongue should confess that Jesus Christ is Lord, to the glory of God the Father.

The book of Revelation goes on to give us a glimpse of when all the kingdoms of this world have become the kingdoms of our Lord and of His Christ. Right now it may not be that way, but it is not over yet.

Revelation 11:15
Then the seventh angel sounded: And there were loud voices in heaven, saying, "The kingdoms of this world have become the kingdoms of our Lord and of His Christ, and He shall reign forever and ever!"

Jesus said that even hell itself does not have enough power to stop the church fulfilling its purpose. Jesus is the master builder, and He is still busy at work finishing the job that He started. He is not finished with you, or your church, family even, and He will accomplish that which He set out to do.

Matthew 16:18
And I also say to you that you are Peter, and on this rock I will build My church, and the gates of Hades shall not prevail against it.

Jesus Victory On The Cross

What seemed to be a great loss, turned out to be just the opposite. When Jesus was betrayed, unjustly accused, and brutally crucified, it seemed as if the disciples' world suddenly fell apart. Three days later the tables were turned and Jesus rose victorious from the grave. Satan's camp was set in confusion, and new hope restored to Jesus' faithful followers. When you are in God's plan, things may seem one way at one moment, but dramatically change in the next. The point is to stand your ground in faith, no matter the circumstances. Jesus will lead you out of the circumstances and cause you to triumph in the end.

2 Corinthians 2:14
Now thanks be to God who always leads us in triumph in Christ...

Your future hinges on whether you understand the authority Jesus already holds in three realms: heaven, on earth and below it. You have a choice to live in the light of His victory which He purchased at the cross, or live in the light of what the circumstances are telling you. He is not subject to change, but circumstances are. Make the choice to side with the higher reality of the eternal truth of God's word.

It Is All A Matter Of Perspective

God has an eternal perspective on everything. What He does, He does forever. However, we are mainly focused on one thing for a while, and then move on the next. God never loses His focus, and He always finishes what He starts. He will fully establish His will on earth, and wants us to play our part in this restoration process. He knows the beginning from the end, and will show us what we need to know, if we ask Him. Even though ultimately we know only in part, the part we know is enough to cause us to be victorious! God has sets things up that way. We have a perspective that satan will never have because we are related to God through Jesus. In Christ we always have the upper hand on our adversary! Do not let him lie to you that he is more powerful than God, or you for that matter. God is all-powerful, and you have personal access to His power, provision and protection through the covenant promises Jesus set in motion when he paid for our redemption at the cross.

Things Are Not Always The Way They Appear

Ever wonder how the weather forecasters can predict thunderstorms will break out in the afternoon when you only see clear skies in the morning. They know (can see) things that you and I do not know. They know the humidity levels, upper air movements etc. It is like they have inside information on the weather. It is like that with the things of God. He reveals His secret counsel to the upright who are in close touch with Him through His Word and prayer.

Proverbs 3:32
For the perverse person is an abomination to the LORD,
But His secret counsel is with the upright.

God's ways are not a mystery to those who call upon Him to understand the what, when, how and why of what is going on in the spirit. We are encouraged to call upon the Lord and ask Him to show us things to come, things that are already in process. If we are in the dark, it is because we simply have not asked!

Jeremiah 33:3
'Call to Me, and I will answer you, and show you great and mighty things, which you do not know.'

Because we only know and prophesy in part, we must have faith that what God is doing is far greater than what we see satan doing. Truth dispels lies, just as light always dispels darkness. As a Christian, you are on the winning team, and in God's book you are destined to succeed despite what contrary circumstances may say.

What the enemy plans for evil, God is able to turn around to our advantage. Satan's plans always backfire when you put your life in the hands of the Lord and trust Him. For example, when the rulers of the day, in their so called wisdom, conspired to crucify Jesus, they thought they had things all wrapped up. The problem was that they were playing into God's hands all along. God had already prophesied that Jesus would rise victorious from the dead and utterly defeat death, hell and the grave.

> 1 Corinthians 2:6-8
> However, we speak wisdom among those who are mature, yet not the wisdom of this age, nor of the rulers of this age, who are coming to nothing. But we speak the wisdom of God in a mystery, the hidden wisdom which God ordained before the ages for our glory, which none of the rulers of this age knew; for had they known, they would not have crucified the Lord of glory.

Satan, who was behind the scenes orchestrating their foolishness, suddenly had the tables turned on his diabolical schemes. Life conquered death, and light overcame the darkness.

God's wisdom is hidden from the disobedient 'rulers of this age', but revealed to us in Christ. Satan does not have access to God's heart, but as God's children we do! We are privy to the secret counsel of His covenant.

Psalm 25:14

The secret of the LORD is with those who fear Him,

And He will show them His covenant.

The Purpose Of This Book

The purpose of this book is to help you understand that the spirit realm is very real and directly affects what is going on in your life at a personal level, as well as on a larger scale in the nation you reside. God's plan requires that you are in tune with Him in His realm, and that you exercise your God given authority in your sphere of influence. When you do, you are guaranteed to win the good fight of faith, bring God the glory He deserves, and fulfill His plan for your life.

When we believe with our hearts, we truly see things with an eternal perspective.

Chapter 2

The Spirit Realm

Introduction

Many people struggle to recognize the existence of a spiritual realm. They only relate to things they can comprehend with their five senses. They struggle to contact God because they cannot figure Him out in their minds, not realizing that faith is a spiritual dynamic of the heart that puts you in touch with the 'unseen' spirit realm.

Perhaps the problem has to do with the society in which they have grown up. Some societies are more in tune with the spirit realm than their more secular counterparts. Yet, in all communities, when you scratch beneath the surface, you find at least some awareness of the unseen spiritual realm. This is shown in tales about ghosts, goblins, and angels that are found in all folklore. Superstition is further proof of an awareness of the spirit realm.

The things of the unseen spirit realm have a direct bearing on life in the same way that gravity as an unseen natural force affects us all. The issue is not whether we can see something or not. 'Seeing' with the natural eye, is not the same as 'believing' with the heart. Rather, it is when we believe with our hearts and that we truly see things with an eternal perspective.

God Is A Spirit, Not A Mind Or Force

John 4:24
God is Spirit, and those who worship Him must worship in spirit and truth."

God is the supreme Spirit being with a definite contactable personality in the spirit. He is not some impersonal force for good. Our worship would make no sense if this were true. You do not worship an inanimate object like a tree or some force, but a living personality. That is why worshipping at a stone or wood pillar, or some other idolatrous object of your own making, is foolish.

The Unseen God Made All Things Seen

God preexisted all things seen and unseen. In fact, He made everything in the universe, both in the material and the spiritual realms. The material realm depends on and is influenced by the spirit realm.

Hebrews 11:3

By faith we understand that the worlds were framed
by the word of God, so that the things which are seen
were not made of things which are visible.

You could say that the spiritual realm directs and determines the material realm, and that all things have a spiritual root. Things in the natural do not exist independently from the spirit. This book explores the connection between the two.

Consider this amazing revelation from God about the connection between the spiritual fall of man and the material and seen realm of creation, which is now waiting for deliverance from the corruption that was introduced through Adam's sin in the garden.

Romans 8:21

... because the creation itself also will be delivered
from the bondage of corruption into the glorious liberty of the children of God. For we know that the
whole creation groans and labors with birth pangs
together until now.

The whole physical creation is waiting for a time when it will be delivered (and restored) from the bondage of corruption. Think of earthquakes, floods, famines, volcanoes and other such violent occurrences. They are the result of a disorder that was imposed on the world through Adam's sin! It is as if the earth is groaning and laboring as it struggles to be free from some sort of imbalance. Why else would God need to create a new heaven and earth, if this 'old' one is OK? The glorious liberty of the children of God is a spiritual reality that is connected to the material realm. When mankind enjoys the full redemption of a new heaven and earth, then all disorder in the natural realm will be set right.

Hidden Forces In The Realm Of The Spirit

Why is it that people are so unreasonable when it comes to racial prejudice, marriage and family betrayal, continued strife in the Middle East, and so on? I believe unseen spiritual forces are at play in the human drama, and when we understand them, and take our stand, we can avoid much confusion, heartache and failure.

Most people live their lives largely dictated to by what they comprehend with their natural senses. They walk in what the Bible calls the 'flesh'. Even God's people do not always walk 'in the spirit'. They do not always fully take advantage of what is available to them. Only when a believer is in tune with God's Spirit, does he begins to see things that are already there in the spirit realm. 'Tuning in' to the wave length of the spirit realm is an essential skill in living with authority.

For example, Elisha and his servant faced overwhelming odds in the natural as they looked out at the army that had been sent by the Syrian king to surround Jerusalem.

2 Kings 6:14-17
Therefore he sent horses and chariots and a great army there, and they came by night and surrounded the city. And when the servant of the man of God arose early and went out, there was an army, surrounding the city with horses and chariots. And his servant said to him, "Alas, my master! What shall we do?" So he answered, "Do not fear, for those who are with us are more than those who are with them." And Elisha prayed, and said, "LORD, I pray, open his eyes that he may see." Then the LORD opened the eyes of the young man, and he saw. And behold, the mountain was full of horses and chariots of fire all around Elisha.

What they saw was a host of God's angels that were **already there** and assigned to defend them against the enemy. Elisha was already in tune with the spirit realm, but his servant was not. Because Elisha saw into the spirit realm, he was not desperately asking God to do something, and panicking in the face of danger. His servant, on the other hand, was panicking. He was reacting to what he saw with his natural eyes.

It is therefore very necessary and scriptural to pray that our 'spiritual' eyes be opened to what God has already done in the spirit realm (Ephesians 1:17-18). When your eyes are open to what God has already set in place, great victories can be won.

The apostle John, who walked closely with Jesus, continued to serve God faithfully right into his old age. He was exiled for his faith on the Isle of Patmos, just off the southwestern coast of modern Turkey. He was a spiritual man, schooled in God's ways, yet in the book of Revelation we read that on the Lord's Day one time, he was 'in the spirit.' This heightened awareness of the spirit realm opened him up to things he had never seen or heard before.

Revelation 1:9-12

I, John, both your brother and companion in the tribulation and kingdom and patience of Jesus Christ, was on the island that is called Patmos for the word of God and for the testimony of Jesus Christ. I was in the Spirit on the Lord's Day, and I heard behind me a loud voice, as of a trumpet, saying, "I am the Alpha and the Omega, the First and the Last," and, "What you see, write in a book and send it to the seven churches which are in Asia: to Ephesus, to Smyrna, to Pergamos, to Thyatira, to Sardis, to Philadelphia, and to Laodicea." Then I turned to see the voice that spoke with me. And having turned I saw seven golden lampstands,

He both heard and saw new things in the spirit. Like John, to step up higher in the things of God you have to position yourself through a lifestyle of diligent worship. John's reward was to see into the future, and even get insight into the majesty of God's throne. He was called to 'come up here', to a place that already existed in the spirit realm.

Revelation 4:1-2
After these things I looked, and behold, a door standing open in heaven. And the first voice which I heard was like a trumpet speaking with me, saying, "Come up here, and I will show you things which must take place after this." Immediately I was in the Spirit; and behold, a throne set in heaven, and One sat on the throne.

It is important to be 'looking' for the things of the spirit. If your heart is right, you will discover what God wants you to see, that which is relevant to your life and purpose.

Created In God's Image, Of His 'Kind'

Genesis 1:26-27

Then God said, "Let Us make man in Our image, according to Our likeness; let them have dominion over the fish of the sea, over the birds of the air, and over the cattle, over all the earth and over every creeping thing that creeps on the earth." So God created man in His own image; in the image of God He created him; male and female He created them.

As we have seen, God is a spirit, and if He has made man in His image, that makes a man a spirit being at his core! Of course, you and I live in a body and possess a soul, but in our essence we are spirit beings!

God has the capacity to think with His mind. He thinks thoughts about us all the time (Jeremiah 29:11). Then in Christ we know that God has a body! Jesus, who is God, became flesh and dwelt among us (John 1:14).

When we read in the New Testament that we are made up of spirit, soul and body, things start to make sense.

1 Thessalonians 5:23

Now may the God of peace Himself sanctify you completely; and may your whole spirit, soul, and body be preserved blameless at the coming of our Lord Jesus Christ.

With our bodies we contact and relate with the material realm by engaging our five senses of touch, taste, sight, hearing, and smell.

Our minds comprehend all these inputs according to our thought patterns or mental understanding of how things work or fit together. With our minds, we also interact with the world of ideas and concepts.

Then, with our spirits we contact and interact with the spirit realm. Our minds may try to make sense of things, but since the fall, the mind needs to be 'renewed' to think in tune with what God has revealed in His Word.

In the end, the totality of our being comes into play in the communication process. Things begin in the spirit, then affect the mental realm and finally the flesh has to line up. If you reverse the process however, God's order is upset. You become ruled by your senses (body) and mind, and not by God's Word which is also spirit.

John 6:63
The words that I speak to you are spirit, and they are life.

The spirit of man, his soul and body are all connected, and it is unwise to artificially compartmentalize them into watertight segments that are not connected. For example, in our worship we are commanded to love God with the totality of our being: spirit, soul and body.

Deuteronomy 6:5

You shall love the LORD your God with all your heart, with all your soul, and with all your strength.

There is a divine order here: spirit (heart) first, then soul, then body. At all times, we must recognize the priority of the spirit realm. This understanding and its implications have to be cultivated before we can enjoy the full benefit of our authority in Christ.

Since The Fall

When Adam and Eve fell from grace in the Garden of Eden, sin and death was introduced into the earth. (Death is defined as a **separation** from the source of life, in this case spiritually from God Himself).

God was motivated by His love to set in motion His plan to restore man to his originally intended position and purpose. This plan is still playing out six thousand years later in our time both on an individual and a global scale.

When we repent and confess Jesus as Lord, our 'spirit man' is born again. The Holy Spirit regenerates our spirit, and we receive a new spiritual nature recreated in God's image, but our minds have to be renewed in a process of transformation. This transformation happens when we present our bodies to the Lord in a lifestyle of discipline.

Romans 12:1-2

...that you present your bodies a living sacrifice, holy, acceptable to God, which is your reasonable service. And do not be conformed to this world, but be transformed by the renewing of your mind ...

Up till the time we are born again, our minds are shaped or molded by the world system, or way of thinking, and serves as an unreliable source of revelation about God and His ways. Only when our thinking is renewed to the Word of God, do we start to understand the spirit realm correctly. So it is vital to continually meditate on God's Word so that your mind can start to think in line with your heart, or spirit man, which is now 'alive' or sensitized to God in the spirit realm.

When this happens, it is as if our spirits, souls and bodies 'fly in formation' with God's Word (which is His will). Harmony is restored, and we begin to enjoy the promised abundant life in Christ.

John 10:10

I have come that they may have life, and that they may have it more abundantly.

Everything that happens is subject to some sort of law, either of the spirit or the natural realm.

Chapter 3

It Is All About Authority

⚜ ⚜

Introduction

The spiritual and physical universe is ordered according to a set of laws. God is not haphazard in the way He does things, and He also abides by His own laws. In the case of miracles, even when natural laws are apparently interrupted, God operates according to the higher laws of the spirit He set in place.

For example, when Jesus walked on water, the natural law of gravity was temporarily suspended or overridden by the higher law of faith in God's Word that Jesus operated in at that moment. He walked on water according to God's promise to be with Him even when He 'passed through the waters' (Isaiah 43:2). He never did anything outside of God's will.

Jesus functioned on earth in His chosen and 'limited' capacity as **a man born** of a virgin and **anointed** by the Holy Spirit to do what He did. He chose to limit His divinity so that He could show us the way as a true human representative. Otherwise, it would be unreasonable and unfair to expect us to live on earth today like He expects us to.

Acts 10:38

…how God anointed **Jesus of Nazareth** with the Holy Spirit and with power, who went about doing good and healing all who were oppressed by the devil, for God was with Him (emphasis added).

The title given here is 'Jesus of Nazareth', emphasizing His human origin, not His divine origin as the eternally existent God. On earth, He subjected Himself to the laws that govern all mankind, but nevertheless accessed God's higher laws through the anointing of the Holy Spirit. He healed the sick, cast out devils, and walked on water in the power of the Spirit.

In no way was He less than fully God, for scripture teaches that 'in Him lived all the fullness of the Godhead bodily' (Colossians 2:9). Yet, as we are taught in Philippians, He 'emptied' Himself of certain divine privileges to function as a man who could identify with man and thus represent man's plight to God as a mediator.

Philippians 2:5-8

Let this mind be in you which was also in Christ Jesus, who, being in the form of God, did not consider it robbery to be equal with God, but made Himself of no reputation, taking the form of a bondservant, and coming in the likeness of men. And being found in appearance as a man, He humbled Himself and became obedient to the point of death, even the death of the cross.

To summarize, everything that happens is subject to law, either of the spirit or the natural realm. A law a 'rule or principle to be followed'. In order to exercise authority, law must be obeyed. Law and authority are closely connected. They go hand in hand. I will go into this in more detail later in this chapter. But first, what happened when Adam sinned, and how did that affect things in the spirit?

Authority Lost... And Regained

God placed Adam and Eve on earth to exercise authority over it. They were to be His under rulers and had been given a 'dominion mandate' over the earth.

Genesis 1:26-28

Then God said, "Let Us make man in Our image, according to Our likeness; let them have dominion over the fish of the sea, over the birds of the air, and over the cattle, over all the earth and over every creeping thing that creeps on the earth." So God created man in His own image; in the image of God He created him; male and female He created them. Then God blessed them, and God said to them, "Be fruitful and multiply; fill the earth and subdue it; have dominion over the fish of the sea, over the birds of the air, and over every living thing that moves on the earth."

The Psalms echo this truth. God has chosen to delegate His authority on earth to His man.

Psalm 8:6
You have made him to have dominion over the works of Your hands;
You have put all things under his feet,

Psalm 115:16
The heaven, even the heavens, are the LORD's;
But the earth He has given to the children of men.

This is consistent with God's creative intent: to make man in His own image and likeness. God has dominion over the universe, and wants to train up His sons and daughters to exercise dominion in their sphere of delegated influence which is the earth. Of course this can only be successful when we are born again, regenerated in Christ, and our minds renewed to His ways. Under His Lordship, we exercise authority in line with God's authority.

God remains earth's creator and owner, but its stewardship has been delegated to mankind: male and female together. Sadly, when Adam sinned he sold out to satan, and death was introduced as a consequence of this original sin.

Spiritual death or 'separation' entered mankind's spiritual lineage first. This was later followed by physical death. Sin separated man's spirit from God, and then the body was separated from the inner man at the point of physical death. Man's nature became corrupt, and fallen man now had no capacity within himself to redeem the situation. That is why Jesus had to be fathered by God through the Holy Spirit in the 'Immaculate Conception' or virgin birth when the angel appeared to the then Virgin Mary. Jesus' blood had to be pure and uncorrupted by sin. His father (or originator of life) had to be God because Joseph's blood was tainted by sin. That is why the virgin birth is essential to the truth.

Through Adam's sin, satan became the illegal 'ruler' or 'god' of the world system, corrupting every person who was thereafter born into the world. The Bible describes him as the 'god of this age' or world system in 2 Corinthians 4:4. The authority Adam had been given by God, was 'lost' to the corrupter, and satan now gained 'dominion' over mankind.

God's plan to rescue, regenerate, restore and release man back to a position of authority unfolded throughout the Old

Testament and came to a climax when Jesus, who took man-kind's sin on Himself on the cross, defeated satan and rose triumphantly from the dead.

When someone submits to Christ's Lordship, he is totally identified as coming under Jesus authority or dominion. Indeed, the believer is 'in Christ' and born again into God's kingdom or dominion.

Because Jesus lived a sinless life perfectly free from satan's influence, He qualified to be given all authority in all realms. He has the right to delegate that authority to whoso-ever He wishes. Matthew and Mark record that Jesus chose to delegate authority to His followers. They were to go in His name to preach the gospel to every creature, and make disciples of all nations.

Matthew 28:18-20

And Jesus came and spoke to them, saying, "All authority has been given to Me in heaven and on earth. Go therefore and make disciples of all the nations, baptizing them in the name of the Father and of the Son and of the Holy Spirit, teaching them to observe all things that I have commanded you; and lo, I am with you always, even to the end of the age." Amen.

Mark 16:15-18

And He said to them, "Go into all the world and preach the gospel to every creature. He who believes and is baptized will be saved; but he who does not believe will be condemned. And these signs will follow those who believe: In My name they will cast out demons; they will speak with new tongues; they will take up serpents; and if they drink anything deadly, it will by no means hurt them; they will lay hands on the sick, and they will recover."

It seems clear that when a believer responds in faith and obedience to this commission, and then goes into the entire world in the name of Jesus, he or she has authority over all forms of evil that might come against them. This authority has its source in Jesus' command, and must be boldly exercised to be effective.

Let's look a little closer at authority and its source.

What Is Authority?

Authority may be defined as the 'lawful permission to exercise power'. It involves two aspects. The lawful permission or 'right' to exercise authority or power, and actual power or might needed to follow through or enforce what is needed. For example, a police officer has both the 'right' or permission to exercise authority, as well as the training, skills, equipment and weaponry, or the 'might' to enforce his authority where needed.

The Bible speaks of these two aspects of authority in the account where Jesus delegated His authority to His disciples while He was training them.

> Luke 9:1-2
> Then He called His twelve disciples together and gave them power and authority over all demons, and to cure diseases. He sent them to preach the kingdom of God and to heal the sick.

Here, both the 'can do, miraculous force' or 'might to do it' **power**, and the 'permission or lawful, privilege' and delegated 'right to do it' **authority** is described by two different Greek words: 'dunamis' and 'exousia'. Jesus delegated both power and authority to His disciples by simply instructing them to go. They responded in faithful obedience, did what they were instructed to do, and the miraculous results followed. The dead were raised, lepers cleansed, and multitudes were healed of all manner of sickness. People were even delivered from demonic possession. This shows that satanic authority is overridden by God's authority operating through believing disciples.

Where Does Authority Come From?

True spiritual authority always comes from God. He created all things, and everything is under His authority. He created all beings in the spiritual realm, angels and heavenly creatures. He also created all things in what we call the material realm, animals, plants etc. Everything spiritual and material is under God's authority. Even civil authority comes from God. The creator has all authority. However, history shows that authority may be illegally usurped and improperly exercised, but ultimately all authority comes from God.

To be in authority you always have to be under some authority. That is why we know that Jesus functioned in His capacity as a man under authority. He was under God's authority, not His own. He only did what He did because He had authority delegated to him by His Father in Heaven.

Matthew 8:9

For I also am a man under authority...

The centurion, who was in authority over his men, derived his military authority because he was under a higher authority. He recognized this principle in Jesus, that He too was a man under authority. Jesus got his authority from God. He was anointed by the Holy Spirit for service and went about exercising authority (Acts 10:38).

Authority and anointing always function together. Jesus could do what He did because He was empowered (anointed) by the Holy Spirit. In addition, not only did Jesus submit to the authority and anointing of the Father and Holy Spirit, He also submitted to the authority of the Word.

Luke 4:16-21

16 So He came to Nazareth, where He had been brought up. And as His custom was, He went into the synagogue on the Sabbath day, and stood up to read. 17 And He was handed the book of the prophet Isaiah. And when He had opened the book, He found the place where it was written:

18 "The Spirit of the LORD is upon Me,
Because He has anointed Me
To preach the gospel to the poor;
He has sent Me to heal the brokenhearted,
To proclaim liberty to the captives
And recovery of sight to the blind,
To set at liberty those who are oppressed;
19 To proclaim the acceptable year of the LORD."

20 Then He closed the book, and gave it back to the attendant and sat down. And the eyes of all who were in the synagogue were fixed on Him. 21 And He began to say to them, "Today this Scripture is fulfilled in your hearing."

It is clear from the above passage that Jesus operated His ministry within the bounds of the already existent Old Testament Word of God! He ministered on the basis of, and also in fulfillment of scripture. After all, He was and still is the 'Living Word'.

For example, when Jesus was with His disciples at the last supper, He spoke of the one who would shortly betray Him by referring to the scripture that foretold of this betrayal.

John 13:18

I do not speak concerning all of you. I know whom I have chosen; but that the Scripture may be fulfilled, 'He who eats bread with Me has lifted up his heel against Me.'

In a second example, Jesus having attracted quite a crowd nevertheless warned the people not to advertise His presence in fulfillment of Isaiah's prophecy.

Matthew 12:15-21

And great multitudes followed Him, and He healed them all. Yet He warned them not to make Him known, that it might be fulfilled which was spoken by Isaiah the prophet, saying:
"Behold! My Servant whom I have chosen,
My Beloved in whom My soul is well pleased!
I will put My Spirit upon Him,

And He will declare justice to the Gentiles.
He will not quarrel nor cry out,
Nor will anyone hear His voice in the streets.
A bruised reed He will not break,
And smoking flax He will not quench,
Till He sends forth justice to victory;
And in His name Gentiles will trust."

We know Jesus was a student of the Word of God. He spent His time interacting with the teachers of the law in the temple at the tender age of twelve as recorded in Luke 2:41-47. It is fair to say that when He warned the people not to 'make Him known' He was conducting His ministry in the light of scripture He already knew. He literally fulfilled scripture wherever He went. He obeyed the commandments of God absolutely, and never sinned. He was totally submitted to God's word, and the depth and power of His authority was recognized as He spoke.

Mark 1:21-22
Then they went into Capernaum, and immediately on the Sabbath He entered the synagogue and taught. And they were astonished at His teaching, for He taught them as one having authority, and not as the scribes.

His authority was also recognized as He performed mighty deeds in the power of the Holy Spirit. There is a strong connection between the doctrine or word He was teaching, and the miraculous power to command unclean demon spirits.

Mark 1:27

Then they were all amazed, so that they questioned among themselves, saying, "What is this? What new doctrine is this? For with authority He commands even the unclean spirits, and they obey Him."

When the leaders of the temple challenged Jesus as to the source of His authority, He acknowledged that His authority was from a source other than Himself. He challenged them to recognize that He operated in the authority from heaven as it was imparted to Him at His baptism through John the Baptist, a recognized prophet in the community.

Matthew 21:23-25

Now when He came into the temple, the chief priests and the elders of the people confronted Him as He was teaching, and said, "By what authority are You doing these things? And who gave You this authority?" But Jesus answered and said to them, "I also will ask you one thing, which if you tell Me, I likewise will tell you by what authority I do these things: The baptism of John—where was it from? From heaven or from men?"

Jesus had just shaken up the ungodly way of doing things in the temple precincts, and violently upset the religious authorities. He was not ministering with their permission. In effect, they questioned His authority. Secure in His authority as the Son of God, He 'played them at their own game', refusing to give revelation knowledge to these unbelieving, rebellious, fearful and envious religious manipulators.

In the ministry, God anoints and stand behind whom He appoints. Man's responsibility is to recognize and cooperate with what God has already done. However, if you go in your own name or authority, and not God's, essentially you are on your own! The sons of Sceva found that out when they tried to cast out devils and got beaten up for their misguided efforts (Acts 19:14). They were not under God's authority, and thus could not exercise authority over the demon.

Authority, Submission And Servant hood

Authority depends on submitting to God and serving His purposes. He delegates authority to His followers who have confessed Jesus as Lord, and who are intent on doing what He has commanded.

Luke 10:1, 17-20

After these things the Lord appointed seventy others also, and sent them two by two before His face into every city and place where He Himself was about to go...

...Then the seventy returned with joy, saying, "Lord, even the demons are subject to us in Your name." And He said to them, "I saw Satan fall like lightning from heaven. Behold, I give you the authority to trample on serpents and scorpions, and over all the power of the enemy, and nothing shall by any means hurt you. Nevertheless do not rejoice in this, that the spirits are subject to you, but rather rejoice because your names are written in heaven."

In this passage, Jesus delegates His authority to the seventy disciples, who go out in His name, later to come back rejoicing that even the demons are subject to them.

However, Jesus has to quickly correct them as to their improper focus. They were more excited about the authority they now had, and less impressed by the fact that they had submitted to Him in relationship. They were rather to rejoice in the fact that their names were written in heaven. Their submission to Him put them in a position to be in authority, and they should always keep that truth central. Jesus sharply reminded them that both the permission and power to do wonders flowed out of their submission to Him.

Jesus' heart was always to serve the needs of mankind. So the exercise of any authority in His name must reflect that same heart motivation. It is not a matter of authority for authority's sake. Authority always has a purpose attached to it. In God's kingdom, authority is given to serve the needs of others, and not to expect, demand or coerce service to the one in authority. Sadly, many ministers use their authority to lord it over people who essentially serve them. Yet Jesus' heart was not to come and be served, but to serve. That is what He was seeking.

Matthew 20:20-28

Then the mother of Zebedee's sons came to Him with her sons, kneeling down and asking something from Him. And He said to her, "What do you wish?" She said to Him, "Grant that these two sons of mine may sit, one on Your right hand and the other on the left, in Your kingdom." But Jesus answered and said, "You do not know what you ask. Are you able to drink the cup that I am about to drink, and be baptized with the baptism that I am baptized with?" They said to Him, "We are able." So He said to them, "You will indeed drink My cup, and be baptized with the baptism that I am baptized with; but to sit on My right hand and on My left is not Mine to give, but it is for those for whom it is prepared by My Father." And when the ten heard it, they were greatly displeased with the two brothers. But Jesus called them to Himself and said, "You know that the rulers of the Gentiles lord it over them, and those who are great exercise authority over them. Yet it shall not be so among you; but whoever desires to become great among you, let him be your servant. And whoever desires to be first among you, let him be your slave— just as the Son of Man did not come to be served, but to serve, and to give His life a ransom for many."

Here, the mother of Zebedee's sons sought a place or a position of authority for her sons. She wanted them to sit in positions of honor: on Jesus' left and right hand. Judging by Jesus' rebuke, she was overly ambitious and out of touch with His heart and mission. The other ten disciples' displeasure indicated that not one of them understood His heart at this point: the essence of authority is serving the needs of others. Jesus contrasted the gentile approach: 'lording it over people' with His heart: serving people.

Ministry is about giving to others, not taking from them.

Authority Has A Jurisdiction Within Limits

Jurisdiction is the sphere in which you are lawfully permitted to exercise your authority. When you cross over into another jurisdiction, like a state or county line, you no longer necessarily have authority in that jurisdiction. For example a police officer has authority to enforce the law in one area, but not another. The boundaries must be respected. Authority has its limits.

When applied to spiritual matters, God has given us jurisdiction over our own body, mind and spirit. He expects us to make choices to promote our own well being in all three areas. We are instructed to keep our spirit man subject to him, think in line with His will, and subjugate our bodies in such a way that His purposes for our lives are promoted.

1 Thessalonians 4:4
...that each of you should know how to possess his own vessel in sanctification and honor...

1 Thessalonians 5:23
Now may the God of peace Himself sanctify you completely; and may your whole spirit, soul, and body be preserved blameless at the coming of our Lord Jesus Christ.

God sanctifies us by teaching us how make daily choices that promote the proper use of our spirits, souls and bodies according to His wisdom contained in His Word. He has created us for His glory and in His likeness and image.

We also have authority over sickness and disease that attacks our bodies. Our bodies are the temple or 'dwelling place' of the Holy Spirit, and we are authorized to 'possess them in all sanctification'. When we live healthy lives and resist sickness and disease, we in effect 'set our bodies aside' or sanctify them for His purposes.

True, this passage comes from the context of sexual purity, but in today's world especially, if you do not conduct yourself with purity, you are most likely to be subject to sexually transmitted diseases and become diseased.

When it comes to family, the principle of jurisdiction also applies. God has ordained a proper order and chain of command in the family. When the members of family yield to this, they enjoy the protection and blessing that order affords. He instituted the family in Genesis, and when Jesus is the head of any family, love will predominate. The family will be the springboard from which family members fulfill their God given destiny.

Yet God's plan for the family is constantly under attack from rebellious members within, and ignorant forces from without. For example, it is God's plan for parents to love, serve, and guide and discipline their children. In turn, children are not to dictate and drive family dynamics. Parents will have to give an account to God for how their own children are raised. Educational 'authorities' will not stand before Him on this, only parents.

We have already seen that believers have been given authority (permission and power) over evil spirits in Jesus name (Mark 16:15-20). However, scripture does not teach the unlimited exercise of authority over evil spirits. The disciples did not empty out the asylums of the day. Even Paul waited for the unction before he cast out the evil spirit in the woman at Ephesus. She had been harassing him for a number of days, but only when the time was right did he cast out the spirit of divination.

> Acts 16:16-18
>
> Now it happened, as we went to prayer, that a certain slave girl possessed with a spirit of divination met us, who brought her masters much profit by fortune-telling. This girl followed Paul and us, and cried out, saying, "These men are the servants of the Most High God, who proclaim to us the way of salvation." And this she did for many days. But Paul, greatly annoyed, turned and said to the spirit, "I command you in the name of Jesus Christ to come out of her." And he came out that very hour.

However, although we have been instructed to exercise that authority in the entire world, it is worth noting that you still have to be led by the Holy Spirit in all ministry endeavors. God has a strategy, and each believer must fit into His big picture plans.

For example, the apostle Paul was forbidden by the Holy Spirit to minister in a particular area. If he had pressed on against the leading of the Holy Spirit, God would not have been obliged to support him or bless his efforts there. Paul would have been out of his jurisdiction and overstepped his limits.

Acts 16:6
Now when they had gone through Phrygia and the region of Galatia, they were forbidden by the Holy Spirit to preach the word in Asia.

It is my contention that many ministers only enjoy limited success, simply because they are not in the right place or area of authority or at the right time. A lot of competition within the Body of Christ would be avoided if we understood the principle of jurisdiction.

Jurisdiction in the local church is limited as well. God appoints local shepherds to tend His local sheep. It is a violation of local authority for another minister to come into town and exercise authority over them without God's sanction. The apostolic guidelines in the Word must be followed.

Paul and Peter recognized their separate jurisdictions. Peter was the apostle to the Jews, and Paul to the Gentiles. They respected the local church leadership as well, and did not throw their 'spiritual weight' around in places where they were not invited. They were led by the Holy Spirit in

51

their ministries. Learn to avoid being presumptuous when you exercise authority.

When ministering to the unsaved, recognize that they still have to exercise their will and choose between right and wrong. You cannot exercise authority over their will through manipulation, because this amounts to witchcraft or ungodly control. Yes, you can and must strongly influence them to submit to Jesus, but you cannot force them. It is the Holy Spirit's ministry to persuade and draw people to Christ. Learn not to overstep the mark as you co labor with Him.

In general, when ministering to people they have to consent to your ministry or give you authority to speak into their lives. They do this by asking for help or prayer, attending your meeting, church service or Bible study. For example, if parents bring a sick child to your meeting for prayer, they authorize you to minister to that child. Otherwise, you do not have free course to do what you will in the situation.

In summary, to successfully exercise authority anywhere, you have to be 'received'. Consider the following example when Jesus gave authority to His disciples. He instructed then to depart from any city where they were not received. However, where they were received, they enjoyed success in their preaching.

Luke 9:1-6
Then He called His twelve disciples together and gave them power and authority over all demons, and

to cure diseases. He sent them to preach the kingdom of God and to heal the sick. And He said to them, "Take nothing for the journey, neither staffs nor bag nor bread nor money; and do not have two tunics apiece. Whatever house you enter, stay there, and from there depart. And whoever will not receive you, when you go out of that city, shake off the very dust from your feet as a testimony against them." So they departed and went through the towns, preaching the gospel and healing everywhere.

Jesus had been ministering in Judea, the region around Jerusalem, but had to go through Samaria on His way back to Galilee. When He arrived back in Galilee, they received Him having earlier experienced His ministry in Jerusalem when they went up for one of the annual feasts.

John 4:43-45
Now after the two days He departed from there and went to Galilee. For Jesus Himself testified that a prophet has no honor in his own country. So when He came to Galilee, the Galileans received Him, having seen all the things He did in Jerusalem at the feast; for they also had gone to the feast.

He was easily able to exercise His authority there and perform miracles in their community because they received Him.

In contrast, His authority was limited by the unbelief of His hometown citizens. Mark's gospel records that He 'could not' do any mighty work there; not '**would** not', but '**could** not'. Perhaps they had become too familiar with His humanity when He grew up in their midst, and could not comprehend where He got His authority from.

Mark 6:1-6

Then He went out from there and came to His own country, and His disciples followed Him. And when the Sabbath had come, He began to teach in the synagogue. And many hearing Him were astonished, saying, "Where did this Man get these things? And what wisdom is this which is given to Him, that such mighty works are performed by His hands! Is this not the carpenter, the Son of Mary, and brother of James, Joses, Judas, and Simon? And are not His sisters here with us?" And they were offended at Him. But Jesus said to them, "A prophet is not without honor except in his own country, among his own relatives, and in his own house." Now He could do no mighty work there, except that He laid His hands on a few sick people and healed them. And He marveled because of their unbelief.

Jesus did not bypass or override the people's will and perform mighty works despite their unwillingness to receive His ministry. Their unbelief 'limited' His authority or freedom to perform any significant miracles. A few sickly folk opened their hearts to Him, and they got their needs met, but the rest did not, even though His power to heal them was available to them all.

God's people even 'limited' God's power through their unbelief according to Psalm 78:41-2. They did not remember His power in delivering them from Egyptian slavery in the Exodus. As a consequence, they wandered in the wilderness till that unbelief was eradicated

To return to Jesus' ministry, on another occasion He was teaching and the religious teachers and Pharisees were attending the meeting. God's power to heal them was also present, but they did not get healed because of their cynical criticism of His ministry. Only the paralyzed man who was let down through the roof by his friends got healed. Jesus forgave this man's sins, and the irate religious leaders questioned His authority to do so.

The faith of the men who brought him broke through the cloud of unbelief in the house, and the man on the bed received his healing to the glory of God.

Luke 5:17-18

Now it happened on a certain day, as He was teaching, that there were Pharisees and teachers of the law sitting by, who had come out of every town of Galilee, Judea, and Jerusalem. And the power of the Lord was present to heal them. Then behold, men brought on a bed a man who was paralyzed, whom they sought to bring in and lay before Him.

Hard as it may seem, religious tradition renders God's Word of no effect. When we realize that God's Word carries authority or power to bring His will to bear in any situation or need, then the seriousness of unbelieving religious tradition cannot be over emphasized. Even though God's Word is sharp and powerful, able to do all that He sends it out to do, its power can be limited by tradition!

Mark 7:13
...making the word of God of no effect through your tradition which you have handed down.

Make it your business to examine whether you have any empty religious tradition that is hindering you. Religious tradition comes from wrong teaching and believing, and will rob you of the blessings that flow from a simple trusting relationship with God who cares about your every need.

In Charge All The Time?

Some people do not respect their limits. Some leaders, who are used to being in authority, find it hard to stop leading at the limit of their sphere of influence. They were born to lead, so it is natural for them to feel compelled to continue doing so wherever they find themselves at all times. This can cause problems when they step over their boundaries and infringe on someone else's authority.

God wants you to recognize who is in authority wherever you go, and function within that. In church life, for example, a pastor does not have authority over another man's wife or that family's children. Nor does a parishioner have permission to dictate to a pastor what kind of car he should or should not drive. Respect and honor are an integral part of God's family. True Christian love must be at the heart of all relationships.

Joseph in Egypt and Daniel in Babylon were both captive to and under the authority of their masters, but they were still able to function within the limits of their respective adverse circumstances. They did not step out of their respective jurisdictions, but functioned to the glory of God within the boundaries given them. Once again, you do not have to be in charge all the time everywhere you go. You can fulfill your destiny even if you find yourself in restrictive circumstances. Learn to be successful wherever you are in life. Joseph did. He was a successful man even when he was a slave. He was even unfairly thrown in prison, yet continued to be successful as he served under authority. God was with Him even when things were tough. Do not let the enemy lie to you that God has left you when things are rough. Know and believe that the authority you have in Christ cannot be put down if you maintain faith.

The power of obedience cannot be underestimated in waging spiritual warfare.

Chapter 4

Spiritual Warfare

There is a lot of hype and sometimes confusion about spiritual warfare. Many Christians seem to fall into one of two extremes. First, they put **too much emphasis** on 'warring in the spirit' or they pay **too little attention** to the wiles of the enemy. God's Word gives us the proper balance on this matter. I have learned to stick to the Word, and not get swayed by fanciful doctrine based on suspect 'experiences'. Either way, satan gains an advantage if we are ignorant of what God has revealed through His Word.

> 2 Corinthians 2:11
> …lest Satan should take advantage of us; for we are not ignorant of his devices.

This chapter focuses on the nature of spiritual warfare, and the next chapter examines how the devil operates, and also how to exercise your God given authority over him. God's plan remains to rescue, regenerate, restore, and release mankind back to the dominion mandate He originally gave them (male and female) as recorded in Genesis 1:26-28. He sent His Son to deliver us from all the power of the enemy and God expects us to know and enjoy the protection He has provided against his attacks.

The Nature Of Spiritual Warfare

First, satan and his demon underlings undoubtedly exist, and they have a distinct nature and operation.

> 1 Peter 5:8-9
> Be sober, be vigilant; because your adversary the devil walks about like a roaring lion, seeking whom he may devour. Resist him, steadfast in the faith, knowing that the same sufferings are experienced by your brotherhood in the world.

Our adversary's nature is to oppose all that is good. He must be resisted otherwise he will run roughshod over you and gain an advantage. Your faith is vital in resisting the devil. When you stand steadfast on your faith, it blocks the enemy's advances. Faith has two main consequences: it pleases God and dispels fear, which is a product of satan's lies and deceit. The book of Ephesians gives a useful over-view of what you need to know in waging spiritual warfare.

It is often described as the Christian's 'Freedom Charta'. It outlines the position, practice and posture we are to adopt in order to enjoy the victory Jesus has already purchased for us at Calvary.

Ephesians Teaches Us About Spiritual Warfare

When you read the whole book of Ephesians God reveals a pattern of three key words that frame the book: sit, walk and stand.

'Sit' describes our **position** in Christ before God and is found in chapters one to three.

'Walk' describes our Christian **practice** as we live out our lives before our fellow man, and is found in chapters four and five.

'Stand' describes the **posture** we are to adopt towards our adversary the devil, and this emphasis is found in chapter six.

I believe there is a divine progression outlined here. You cannot effectively walk out your Christian faith if you do not know where you are seated. So too, you cannot stand against the enemy unless you have consistently walked out your faith before your fellow man.

Sit

To be successful in spiritual warfare, you have to receive by faith all that Christ has already done for you. He has seated you with Himself at the right hand of God, far above all the powers of the enemy. You are now in a **position of authority** by what Jesus has already done through the cross.

Ephesians 2:1-6

And you He made alive, who were dead in trespasses and sins, in which you once walked according to the course of this world, according to the prince of the power of the air, the spirit who now works in the sons of disobedience, among whom also we all once conducted ourselves in the lusts of our flesh, fulfilling the desires of the flesh and of the mind, and were by nature children of wrath, just as the others. But God, who is rich in mercy, because of His great love with which He loved us, even when we were dead in trespasses, made us alive together with Christ (by grace you have been saved), and raised us up together, and made us sit together in the heavenly places in Christ Jesus,

The last part of the passage describes our position In Christ. We are seated 'together with Jesus in heavenly places'. Our priority is to 'sit' at His feet in this position of authority. When you 'sit down', you are effectively at rest and in faith. You have stopped striving in your own strength, and fully trust in God alone. The first step in spiritual warfare therefore, is to discover through God's word who you are in Christ! In Christ, we are chosen, forgiven, loved, accepted, empowered, and delivered from all the power of the enemy.

Colossians 1:13-14
He has delivered us from the power of darkness and conveyed us into the kingdom of the Son of His love, in whom we have redemption through His blood, the forgiveness of sins.

The **prayer focus** is to pray for **'enlightenment'** as to our position or authority in Him. We must pray for this enlightenment because we do not automatically know who we are in Christ. I have met many Christians, genuinely born again, but almost totally ignorant of who they are in Christ, and the authority they have by virtue of their position. They live defeated lives as a consequence. Paul prays...

Ephesians 1:17-21
...that the God of our Lord Jesus Christ, the Father of glory, may give to you the spirit of wisdom and revelation in the knowledge of Him, the eyes of your understanding being enlightened; that you may know what is the hope of His calling, what are the riches of the glory of His inheritance in the saints, and what

is the exceeding greatness of His power toward us who believe, according to the working of His mighty power which He worked in Christ when He raised Him from the dead and seated Him at His right hand in the heavenly places, far above all principality and power and might and dominion, and every name that is named, not only in this age but also in that which is to come.

He prayed this prayer of enlightenment on behalf of the Ephesian church who obviously needed this prayer. You should pray this prayer for yourself and other Christians. Personalize the prayer and pray it regularly over your life and that of your loved ones. Even pray it over your leadership and friends in the body of Christ. The expected action implied in this prayer is to receive everything by faith. Faith is not a struggle but rather a yielded surrender to God's promised provision. For example, a drowning man must stop struggling in order for someone to save him. He must accept that he is helpless, and must yield to the help he is given by the life saver. In the same way, as Christians we are to simply accept that we cannot save ourselves, let alone wage spiritual warfare against an ancient and wily foe.

Ephesians 2:8-9

For by grace you have been saved through faith, and that not of yourselves; it is the gift of God, not of works, lest anyone should boast.

Spiritual warfare begins from a lofty position of rest, and does not involve sweating it through a 'works program' to get to a position of authority. The fact is you are already there by virtue of the completed work of Christ!

Your adversary will do anything to contradict God's Word. He will try to convince you that you are not worthy to receive this glorious position at God's right hand. Remind him that you have received all that you are by faith, and that your position has nothing to do with whether you have earned it or not.

Walk

Spiritual warfare also involves bearing outwardly God's inward stamp. What you 'live out', must, of necessity, be on the inside first. Here the priority is to 'work out' what has already been 'worked in'. Begin your faith walk with a big 'done', and not a big 'to do' list. We are exhorted to walk 'worthy of our calling'; to 'no longer walk as the rest of the gentiles walk'; 'walk in love'; 'walk in the light'; and 'walk circumspectly', or walk 'with wisdom'. Read Ephesians chapter Four and Five to see all references to 'walk'. When you begin to take steps to walk in all these requirements, you will need God's constant help and strength. He has promised to be by your side, but requires that you pray for His fullness to come forth in your life by His Spirit. Once again the apostle Paul prays for the believers in Ephesus that they might have **the strength** they needed. It was not automatically theirs; it came as a consequence of believing prayer.

Ephesians 3:14-19
For this reason I bow my knees to the Father of our Lord Jesus Christ, from whom the whole family in heaven and earth is named, that He would grant you, according to the riches of His glory, to be strengthened with might through His Spirit in the inner man, that Christ may dwell in your hearts through faith; that you, being rooted and grounded in love, may be able to comprehend with all the saints what is the width and length and depth and height— to know the love of Christ which passes knowledge; that you may be filled with all the fullness of God.

When you have the strength to live out your faith, and are rooted and grounded in God's love (which never fails and is thus the greatest force on earth), then your adversary is rendered powerless. A solid Christian lifestyle of obedience is a sure defense against the enemy. In fact, the more you obey the Lord, the less you obey the enemy. His authority over you weakens with every act of obedience. The power of obedience cannot be underestimated in waging spiritual warfare. God's Word teaches that our enemies are subdued when we walk in obedience. This makes sense as the devil is the author of all disobedience and rebellion.

Psalm 81:13-14
"Oh, that My people would listen to Me,
That Israel would walk in My ways!
I would soon subdue their enemies,
And turn My hand against their adversaries.

Then again, when we listen to God and not the whisperings of the enemy we will dwell safely!

Proverbs 1:33
But whoever listens to me will dwell safely,
And will be secure, without fear of evil."

The above two passages do not emphasize practicing some weird form of spiritual warfare face to face with the enemy in some crude fleshly endeavor, but rather living right before God. Focus your attention on God through praise and worship; and obey His Word. This will quickly sideline the adversary.

Stand

Once a battle has been fought and territory won, only a 'standing' army is required to enforce the victory. A third key facet of spiritual warfare involves standing your ground against the enemy who will come to try to displace you from the position you already occupy!

If you adopt a mindset that you have to fight to gain territory, rather than claim, keep or protect what you already have, then you will be expending unnecessary spiritual energy fighting an unnecessary battle. We already have the victory through Jesus! We need to know it, walk in it and stand against the lies and temptations of the enemy. Temptation only makes sense if you already have what the enemy wants. The priority here is to fight the good fight of faith from a position of victory, not towards a position of victory.

> Ephesians 6:10-11
>
> Finally, my brethren, be strong in the Lord and in the power of His might. Put on the whole armor of God, that you may be able to stand against the wiles of the devil.

God's armor protects you. The only action you are expected to take is to stand your ground. Spiritual warfare has to do with practicing truth, righteousness, peace, walking by faith, and speaking the Word in the face of adverse situations. It is certainly not about shouting at the devil in the flesh. Keep your eyes fixed on Jesus, make it your business to live right, and refuse to allow the enemy's lies to get to your heart. In this way you hold on to the ground you already have in the Lord.

Ephesians 6:13-20

Therefore take up the whole armor of God, that you may be able to withstand in the evil day, and having done all, to stand. Stand therefore, having girded your waist with truth, having put on the breastplate of righteousness, and having shod your feet with the preparation of the gospel of peace; above all, taking the shield of faith with which you will be able to quench all the fiery darts of the wicked one. And take the helmet of salvation, and the sword of the Spirit, which is the word of God; praying always with all prayer and supplication in the Spirit, being watchful to this end with all perseverance and supplication for all the saints— and for me, that utterance may be given to me, that I may open my mouth boldly to make known the mystery of the gospel, for which I am an ambassador in chains; that in it I may speak boldly, as I ought to speak.

Most of our armor is defensive, only the sword being clearly a weapon of offense. A total of six parts of armor are described in the above passage: the girdle or belt of truth; a breastplate of righteousness; shoes of peace; the shield of faith; a helmet of salvation and the sword of the spirit – which is the Word of God. Each piece of the armor must be appropriated and used in faith. They are all spiritual weapons.

For example, if the adversary tries to tell you that you are a no good failure, or an accident going somewhere to happen, refuse to agree with his lies. Take the thoughts captive to the obedience of Christ and in faith declare what God says about you. You are the righteousness of God in Christ, and He has set you on a path of victory in Him. In this way you will guard your heart, speak the truth and step into God's plan for your life. This is the victory in spiritual warfare. Here the **prayer focus** is to ask that God grant you the **boldness to continue speaking the truth (utterance)** in the face of a spiritual attack.

Many Christians stop speaking the Word when they come under attack. In fact, they even begin to question whether the Word still works in their lives. When this happens, the enemy gains an advantage and exploits the doubt and unbelief that inevitably follows such an abdication of authority. God's Word is sharp and powerful, and He watches over His promises to perform them in our lives. We are required to stand our ground and boldly declare the victory we already have by faith in Christ. Hold fast to your confession of faith with all patience. 'Do not let the dog steal your bone'!

What About Wrestling With The Enemy?

Ephesians 6:12

For we do not wrestle against flesh and blood, but against principalities, against powers, against the rulers of the darkness of this age, against spiritual hosts of wickedness in the heavenly places.

Once again, the question you must ask yourself is this: 'Am I wrestling (or fighting) to gain territory or to keep what I already have?' Sure, there is a labor or effort required to enter into the peace of a faith rest, but the wrestling spoken of in verse twelve is not to overcome evil spirits in spiritual warfare, but to resist their attacks against the position you already hold.

In the same way as we are encouraged to 'run' a spiritual race, Paul uses an athletic image (wrestling) to describe the effort it takes to stand your ground against the enemy who contests the stand you have taken. Do not fall into the error of praying all sorts of 'warring prayers' against evil spirits. First, prayer is always directed to God and never to satan. We are supposed to exercise authority over satan, not shout at him in so called 'warfare prayer'. The way in which you exercise authority is to boldly declare God's Word in the circumstances you face, and command satan to leave. Truth always dispels lies, as light always dispels darkness. The only time you address satan and evil spirits is when you command them to leave. Learn to consistently speak out God's Word to enforce satan's defeat as you stand on the ground Jesus has purchased for you!

The Battleground Of The Mind

The Word instructs us to wear the 'helmet of salvation'. Helmets guard the mind. The thoughts you think are vital in spiritual warfare, because they connect what you believe in your heart with what you do with your body. If you think in line with your heart, then the 'flesh' and its appetites have to line up with God's Word. Satan has no room to operate in this kind of environment.

There is much confusion about 'strongholds'. Some contend that they refer to evil spirits that rule in particular geographical areas. They say that in order to enjoy spiritual breakthroughs, these strongholds must be pulled down. So they go to war against these spirits and 'pull them down' through so called intercessory prayer. However, scripture does not support these claims. Consider the following passage in full.

2 Corinthians 10:3-6

For though we walk in the flesh, we do not war according to the flesh. For the weapons of our warfare are not carnal but mighty in God for pulling down strongholds, casting down arguments and every high thing that exalts itself against the knowledge of God, bringing every thought into captivity to the obedience of Christ, and being ready to punish all disobedience when your obedience is fulfilled.

Yes, the passage speaks of spiritual warfare, weapons and strongholds, but it also speaks of 'arguments' and 'high things' that exalt themselves against the knowledge of God. When you consider this additional part to the reference, I believe this scripture teaches that these strongholds refer to 'mental mindsets' rather than evil spirits. We do know, however, that evil spirits move on unsuspecting people to teach 'doctrines' that affect people's way of thinking (1Timothy 4:1). The strongholds are found in people's thinking.

2 Corinthians 4:3-4
But even if our gospel is veiled, it is veiled to those who are perishing, whose minds the god of this age has blinded, who do not believe, lest the light of the gospel of the glory of Christ, who is the image of God, should shine on them.

Here, satan blinds the minds of the unbelieving. He operates in the mind realm injecting lies that divert men from the truth. Doubt is the weapon he introduced to Eve's mind in the original day of temptation, and he is still using the same tactic today. He continues to seek dominion over mankind as the illegitimate 'god' of this age through the flesh and mind.

When someone accepts a lie as the 'truth', they become subject to that falsehood, and the beginnings of a mental stronghold takes root. Lies have a habit of congregating together in clumps, like logs in a river logjam. These lies then stand against God's truth as a stronghold, and have to be 'pulled down'. Every wayward thought has to be brought into captivity to God's Word which is the ultimate truth on any matter under question. I have found it useful to take something that God reveals to me through His Word and use it against thoughts that attack my mind. I quote out loud God's Word as it applies to the negative thought, and declare the Word to be higher authority than the contrary thought. In this way I bring the thought 'captive' to the word of God.

Learn not to lean towards your mental 'reason'. Reasoning is not reasonable when it conflicts with scripture. Jesus taught this when He approached the disciples on the road to Emmaus after he was crucified. He had already been resurrected, but they were walking away from their destiny, and were trying to reason through the weekends traumatic events in their minds. The more they reasoned, the further they got from God's will for their lives. So Jesus came alongside these discouraged disciples, and opened their understanding of the truth of what had happened by means of the scripture.

Luke 24:13-15
Now behold, two of them were traveling that same day to a village called Emmaus, which was about

seven miles from Jerusalem. And they talked together of all these things which had happened. So it was, while they conversed and reasoned, that Jesus Himself drew near and went with them.

Luke 24:25-27

Then He said to them, "O foolish ones, and slow of heart to believe in all that the prophets have spoken! Ought not the Christ to have suffered these things and to enter into His glory?" And beginning at Moses and all the Prophets, He expounded to them in all the Scriptures the things concerning Himself.

It was their own thinking or reasoning that led them astray, and it was an anointed proclamation of scripture that finally gained entrance to their thinking. When the Holy Spirit burned Jesus' word into them, they got back on track. The battlefield is therefore in the mind realm. Satan was attempting to 'blind' their minds once again. Jesus came to their rescue with the Word. It is therefore imperative that your way of thinking be renewed to God's Word. The more you think in line with God's Word, the more your life changes as mental strongholds are 'pulled down'. If you cling to an old way of thinking, God's plan is hindered, and the enemy exploits your ignorance and lack of repentance. After all, 'repentance' means to turn around or change in your way of thinking after the facts of God's truth have been revealed to you.

Romans 12:2
And do not be conformed to this world, but be transformed by the renewing of your mind, that you may prove what is that good and acceptable and perfect will of God.

The Power And Authority In God's Word

When you boldly agree with and declare what God says about you in His Word, then a shift occurs in the spirit realm. God's Word is in itself 'spirit' according to John 6:63, and is described as a 'sword' in the mouth of faith filled believer (Ephesians 6:17). A sword is only useful when it is unsheathed and properly wielded in battle. In spiritual warfare, the enemy is resisted (James 4:7-8) as you speak out God's promises. Jesus did it, and so should you (Luke 4:4 / 6:40).

A nice Bible on the shelf only gathers dust. It must be taken off the shelf, studied, meditated upon (thought about) and spoken into relevant situations or challenges. Then, and then only, does it become powerful and sharp, able to do what God sent it out to do.

Hebrews 4:12

12 For the word of God is living and powerful, and sharper than any two-edged sword, piercing even to the division of soul and spirit, and of joints and marrow, and is a discerner of the thoughts and intents of the heart.

When you live your life and 'go' into your world of influence in His name boldly speaking His Word, in effect you are exercising the authority He has given you. He has said He will back you up with the necessary power or might to bring His will to pass. The Great Commission is great because God is with you to ensure that anything you do in His name produces results.

Mark 16:15-18

15 And He said to them, "Go into all the world and preach the gospel to every creature. 16 He who believes and is baptized will be saved; but he who does not believe will be condemned. 17 And these signs will follow those who believe: In My name they will cast out demons; they will speak with new tongues; 18 they will take up serpents; and if they drink anything deadly, it will by no means hurt them; they will lay hands on the sick, and they will recover."

The supernatural power of God is released when we do what He says: preach or proclaim the good news and do the 'stuff': cast out devils, lay hands on the sick ... in effect take back from the enemy what he has stolen from mankind. When you walk in this, you are engaging in spiritual warfare and recapturing lost ground. God has placed supreme value on His Word, and to do anything else in our lives is only ignorant or foolish.

Psalm 138:2

For You have magnified Your word above all Your name.

He has also promised that His Word will not come back to Him without accomplishing what he sent it out to do.

Isaiah 55:11

11 So shall My word be that goes forth from My mouth;

But it shall accomplish what I please,

And it shall prosper in the thing for which I sent it.

God's Word profits you when you mix faith with it. Empty mouthing does not help you or God in any spiritual battle. In fact, your salvation even depends on a faith confession of your trust in the finished work of Christ on the cross.

Hebrews 4:2-3

For indeed the gospel was preached to us as well as
to them; but the word which they heard did not profit
them, not being mixed with faith in those who heard
it.

Romans 10:9-11

9 that if you confess with your mouth the Lord Jesus
and believe in your heart that God has raised Him
from the dead, you will be saved. 10 For with the
heart one believes unto righteousness, and with the
mouth confession is made unto salvation.

Be fully convinced that God's Word is absolutely crucial
in fighting the good fight of faith. Believe it, speak it and see
it come to pass as you stand your ground. God is waiting for
you to exercise your authority in this way. He will not force
you, nor will he do it for you. It is your responsibility. Do
not let the enemy confuse or distract you into unscriptural
warfare tactics. Stick to the Word.

Angels are ministering spirits that help you do what you have to do. Their God given task includes not only ministering 'to' the saints in their own need, but also 'for' or on behalf of them in their ministry to other people in their need.

Chapter 5

Know Your Friends

Introduction

In any conflict, it sure helps to know who your trusted friends are. Not only has God given us His Holy Spirit to help us in fulfilling His purposes on the earth, but He has commissioned ministering spirits or angels to help and protect us.

> Hebrews 1:13-14
> But to which of the angels has He ever said:
> "Sit at My right hand,
> Till I make Your enemies Your footstool"?
> Are they not all ministering spirits sent forth to minister for those who will inherit salvation?

Angels are ministering spirits that help you do what you have to do. Their God given task includes not only ministering 'to' the saints in their own need, but also 'for' or on behalf of them in their ministry to other people in their need.

What And Who Are Angels?

Angels are not cute bare bottomed 'cupids' with little butterfly like wings as depicted on some Valentine's Day cards. They are not effeminate and weak, nor are they the special property of 'New Age' cults. With so much revived interest today in angels it is useful to know what the Bible has to say about God's angels.

Angels are created spirit beings, generally unseen and invisible to the natural eye. They are most commonly sent by God as **messengers or bearers** of His will. At times they appear in dreams and can also be seen by the natural eye. They can even be entertained unawares at your home (Hebrews 13:2). Although not a common set of experiences for most, we should nevertheless be open to what God does through angels.

Like all else in the spirit realm, we accept their existence and ministry by faith in God's Word.

Rank And Order Among God's Angels

God's angels have a rank, and are ordered in classes to serve specific functions.

1 Peter 3:21-22

...through the resurrection of Jesus Christ, who has gone into heaven and is at the right hand of God, angels and authorities and powers having been made subject to Him.

Colossians 1:16

For by Him all things were created that are in heaven and that are on earth, visible and invisible, whether thrones or dominions or principalities or powers. All things were created through Him and for Him.

The thrones, dominions, authorities, powers and principalities here refer to God's angels, and not satan's under rulers. (Satan counterfeits order and ranking in his own kingdom: We will look into this more later on in another chapter).

For example, in God's realm there are:

- Cherubim: living creatures close to the throne and altar. Genesis 3:24 / Revelation 4:6

- Seraphim: 'burning ones' with wings above the throne. Isaiah 6:6-7

- Archangels. There is only one direct mention of Michael as an Archangel. 1 Thessalonians 4:16

- Angels: with overseeing and warring capabilities. Daniel 10:21 / Revelation 12:7-9

- Gabriel: 'the mighty one' bearing tidings of God's great purposes. Luke 1:13, 19, 26-38

- Ministering spirits: sent to minister for the saints. Hebrews 1:14

It is comforting to know that God's kingdom involves an order and structure where His bidding is carried out by angels of various class and rank. They never contradict or compete with each other. They consistently reveal and bring to pass only His will.

Psalm 103:20-21
Bless the LORD, you His angels,
Who excel in strength, who do His word,
Heeding the voice of His word.
Bless the LORD, all you His hosts,
You ministers of His, who do His pleasure.

They are strong, can and do bless the Lord, and always do His Word and His pleasure.

In contrast, satan is the author of confusion, and though he tries to counterfeit God's order in his domain, he is not

God, and his camp is fatally flawed in its organization and operation.

What Are Angels For?

#1 Angels minister to and on behalf of God.

Angels are constantly worshipping God around His throne.

Revelation 7:11-12
All the angels stood around the throne and the elders
and the four living creatures, and fell on their faces
before the throne and worshiped God, saying:
"Amen! Blessing and glory and wisdom,
Thanksgiving and honor and power and might,
Be to our God forever and ever.
Amen."

They also act as sentinels or protective guards at the heavenly city Jerusalem gates.

Revelation 21:12
Also she had a great and high wall with twelve gates,
and twelve angels at the gates...

I believe our angels in like manner stand guard at the 'gates of our cities' or dwelling places. When Christians in a household, neighborhood, city, region and nation exercise faith in God to occupy, bind the enemy and stand their ground, God's angels hearken to this and assist the believer as sentinels against the enemy's intrusion. At night, I pray and thank God that His angels stand guard over my household as I sleep.

The Bible teaches that an angel will bind up the devil for a thousand years at the end of the age.

Revelation 20:1-3
Then I saw an angel coming down from heaven, having the key to the bottomless pit and a great chain in his hand. He laid hold of the dragon, that serpent of old, who is the Devil and Satan, and bound him for a thousand years; and he cast him into the bottomless pit, and shut him up, and set a seal on him, so that he should deceive the nations no more till the thousand years were finished...

Note that it will take just one angel, seemingly not even an archangel, to deal with the devil at this time. The devil is not as powerful as he would want us to believe. He is only able to deceive nations through his lies and deception. When the truth is told, he cannot stand in its way for one second. Truth always dispels a lie, just as light always dispels darkness.

#2 Angels ministered to and for Jesus.

Angels have and will minister to and for Jesus in the following ways. First, they ministered to Him after the temptations in the wilderness.

> Matthew 4:10-11
> Then Jesus said to him, "Away with you, Satan! For it is written, 'You shall worship the LORD your God, and Him only you shall serve.'" Then the devil left Him, and behold, angels came and ministered to Him.

To minister means to 'serve someone in their need'. Jesus was functioning as the son of man facing temptations as a man, and so He needed angelic support at this time. This can be seen more clearly when an angel strengthened Him as He prepared Himself for the cross in the garden of Gethsemane the night He was betrayed.

> Luke 22:40-43
> When He came to the place, He said to them, "Pray that you may not enter into temptation." And He was withdrawn from them about a stone's throw, and He

knelt down and prayed, saying, "Father, if it is Your will, take this cup away from Me; nevertheless not My will, but Yours, be done." Then an angel appeared to Him from heaven, strengthening Him.

In similar manner **we can expect** God's angels to minister to us in times of temptation and great trial.

When we turn to the future, angels will accompany Jesus at His triumphant return.

Matthew 16:27

For the Son of Man will come in the glory of His Father with His angels, and then He will reward each according to his works.

His angels will also assist Him in separating out good from evil on the Day of Judgment:

Matthew 13:30, 39-42

Let both grow together until the harvest, and at the time of harvest I will say to the reapers, "First gather together the tares and bind them in bundles to burn them, but gather the wheat into my barn."

The enemy who sowed them is the devil, the harvest is the end of the age, and the reapers are the angels. Therefore as the tares are gathered and burned in the fire, so it will be at the end of this age. The Son of Man will send out His angels, and they will gather out of His kingdom all things that offend, and those who practice lawlessness, and will cast them into the furnace of fire...

#3 Angels minister to and for us on earth and in heaven.

Old Testament Examples

Both the Old and New Testaments are full of examples of angelic ministry to and on behalf of the saints. Here are some examples.

Angels were the agency by which the Law was given to Moses on Mount Sinai when the Jews were headed towards the Promised Land. Moses was the mediator of that covenant, and it was appointed through angels.

Galatians 3:19

What purpose then does the law serve? It was added because of transgressions, till the Seed should come to whom the promise was made; and it was appointed through angels by the hand of a mediator.

The angel of the Lord gave Gideon the perspective he needed to break out of his confinement. The angel told Gideon how God saw him. He gave him a fresh perspective: he was in God's sight a mighty man of valor. At this point,

Gideon was fearfully hiding in a winepress trying to thresh a wheat crop. Gideon functioned under these limitations, but God saw things differently and sent an angel to bring Gideon up to a new level. It is always best to be in the right place doing the right thing, and not in the wrong place (wine press) trying to do the right thing (threshing wheat)!

> Judges 6:11-12
>
> Now the Angel of the LORD came and sat under the terebinth tree which was in Ophrah, which belonged to Joash the Abiezrite, while his son Gideon threshed wheat in the winepress, in order to hide it from the Midianites. And the Angel of the LORD appeared to him, and said to him, "The LORD is with you, you mighty man of valor!"

When next you feel downtrodden, think of Gideon and the angel. If an angel appeared to you, what would he say? I believe he would remind you of who you are in Christ and the authority you have in Him. He would encourage you to rise to your true position in Christ and step out and do what God has called you to do.

In the another example, an angel of the Lord ministered instruction to the prophet Elijah when approached by a captain from wicked King Ahaziah's captain for the third time. The first two times the company of fifty men and their captains had been consumed by fire, so it was reasonable at this point, to assume that Elijah was not to go with the third party. Yet an angel was sent to instruct him to go.

It takes faith to hear from God each step of the way. Things change over time, and it is wrong to presume things in walking with God. We are to vigilantly maintain sensitivity to the voice of the Lord, even when it seems contrary to what has previously happened up to this point.

> 2 Kings 1:15
> And the angel of the LORD said to Elijah, "Go down with him; do not be afraid of him." So he arose and went down with him to the king.

In this next example, an angel appeared to Samson's mother announcing his birth and giving her instruction as to how she should live, and how to raise Samson as a consecrated Nazarite. He was to live under a vow of separation for God's purposes.

> Judges 13:2-5
> Now there was a certain man from Zorah, of the family of the Danites, whose name was Manoah; and his wife was barren and had no children. And the Angel of the LORD appeared to the woman and said to her, "Indeed now, you are barren and have borne no children, but you shall conceive and bear a son. Now therefore, please be careful not to drink wine

or similar drink, and not to eat anything unclean. For behold, you shall conceive and bear a son. And no razor shall come upon his head, for the child shall be a Nazirite to God from the womb; and he shall begin to deliver Israel out of the hand of the Philistines."

In yet another example of angelic ministry, when the prophet Balaam's disobedience angered God, an angel of the Lord was sent to stand in Balaam's way and oppose his foolishness.

Numbers 22:22-23
Then God's anger was aroused because he went, and the Angel of the LORD took His stand in the way as an adversary against him. And he was riding on his donkey, and his two servants were with him. 23 Now the donkey saw the Angel of the LORD standing in the way with His drawn sword in His hand, and the donkey turned aside out of the way and went into the field.

Then in Elijah's ministry, an angel was sent to encourage him in time of deep despair. He was being tempted with suicidal thoughts. He had come down from a mighty victory over the false prophets of Baal on Mt Carmel, but was now under a death threat from wicked queen Jezebel. He fled to the wilderness, and it was here in that place of isolation and loneliness that the angel ministered to him, touching him and bringing him food that supernaturally sustained him for forty days and nights.

1 Kings 19:4-8

But he himself went a day's journey into the wilder-ness and came and sat down under a broom tree. And he prayed that he might die, and said, "It is enough! Now, LORD, take my life, for I am no better than my fathers!" Then as he lay and slept under a broom tree, suddenly an angel touched him, and said to him, "Arise and eat." Then he looked, and there by his head was a cake baked on coals, and a jar of water. So he ate and drank, and lay down again. And the angel of the LORD came back the second time, and touched him, and said, "Arise and eat, because the journey is too great for you." So he arose, and ate and drank; and he went in the strength of that food forty days and forty nights as far as Horeb, the mountain of God.

Expect the Lord to send angels to minister to you when you experience deep despair. Right now if you have felt sui-cidal, call upon the Lord and expect Him to send His angels to encourage you.

The Lord's angel in the lion's den protected the prophet Daniel because he was found innocent before the Lord and had done no wrong to the king. When you honor God and respect civil authorities angelic protection is invoked on your behalf in times of threat and danger. A holy life always has its rewards!

Daniel 6:22

My God sent His angel and shut the lions' mouths, so that they have not hurt me, because I was found innocent before Him; and also, O king, I have done no wrong before you."

Daniel's consecration later attracted further angelic intervention as he sought God for understanding of His will.

Angels are given at times by God to reveal heavenly realities to God's people, which are then explained by the Holy Spirit. They work in harmony with God to bring His people to the point of victory.

Zechariah 6:1-5, 9-10

Then I turned and raised my eyes and looked, and behold, four chariots were coming from between two mountains, and the mountains were mountains of bronze. With the first chariot were red horses, with the second chariot black horses, with the third chariot white horses, and with the fourth chariot dappled horses—strong steeds. Then I answered and said to the angel who talked with me, "What are these, my lord?" And the angel answered and said to me, "These are four spirits of heaven, who go out from their station before the Lord of all the earth...

...Then the word of the LORD came to me, saying: "Receive the gift from the captives..."

First, the angel came to the prophet and spoke with him, then the 'word of the Lord' – a reference to the ministry of the Holy Spirit, came to him giving him further instruction.

Do not see the above examples as irrelevant stories applying only to characters in the Bible long time ago. They are given to encourage us in our faith in modern times!

1 Corinthians 10:11

11 Now all these things happened to them as examples, and they were written for our admonition, on whom the ends of the ages have come.

New Testament Examples

To turn to some New Testament examples, we see that angels are as active as they have ever were in the Old Testament.

First, an angel spoke prophetically to Zechariah about His wife and their son to be, John the Baptist (Luke 1:11-20). Zechariah even talked to the angel.

The angel Gabriel was sent to the then virgin Mary announcing the conception, birth and ministry of Jesus the Messiah (Luke 1:26-38). She also talked to this angel.

An angel appeared to Mary's betrothed Joseph in a dream comforting him that Mary's pregnancy was by the Holy Spirit. The angel shared scripture with him, underscoring the vital importance for us today of checking out any angelic visitation or ministry in the light of scripture. (Matthew 1:18-24). The angel also commanded him, and he obeyed.

When Jesus was born, an angel announced the good news to the shepherds. (Luke 2:9-15). Later when the wise men from the East came to worship the Messiah and Herod wanted to kill Jesus, an angel warned Joseph in a dream to flee to Egypt with his wife and child (Matthew 2:12-15). Then again an angel told Joseph in another dream to return, because Herod had died and all was now safe. Before they actually arrived back, he had yet another dream and heard another angelic message warning them not to stop off and stay in Judea near Jerusalem (Matthew 2:19-23).

An angel of the Lord moved the stone away from the entrance to the tomb at Jesus resurrection. This proves they are strong and can directly impact the natural realm (Matthew 28:2-8). The angel is described with a countenance like 'lightning' and his clothing white as snow. The 'Shekinah' glory presence of God was upon the angel as he gave instructions to the two women to go tell Jesus' disciples the good news of His resurrection.

Later, the book of Acts records more angelic activity. An angel gave the evangelist Philip specific direction in his ministry telling him to go down to a deserted place on the trade and travel route that ran from the East through Palestine to Africa.

Acts 8:26-32

Now an angel of the Lord spoke to Philip, saying, "Arise and go toward the south along the road which goes down from Jerusalem to Gaza." This is desert. So he arose and went. And behold, a man of Ethiopia, a eunuch of considerable authority under Candace the queen of the Ethiopians, who had charge of all her treasury, and had come to Jerusalem to worship, 28 was returning. And sitting in his chariot, he was reading Isaiah the prophet. Then the Spirit said to Philip, "Go near and overtake this chariot." So Philip ran to him, and heard him reading the prophet Isaiah, and said, "Do you understand what you are reading?" And he said, "How can I, unless someone guides me?" And he asked Philip to come up and sit with him. The place in the Scripture which he read was this: ...

In this divine appointment we see the divine cooperation between Philip's obedience, an angel, and the Holy Spirit.

See also how Philip uses the scripture to meet the Ethiopian Eunuch's need.

Then, there are records of numerous angelic encounters throughout church history right up to our modern day. There is no Bible reference to their work ever having ceased. Unfortunately, many believers in the body of Christ discount the supernatural. Filled with 'religious unbelief' they invoke their own self fulfilling 'prophecies' and never experience God's provision in this area. They actually limit God's operation in their lives by discounting and not expecting God's supernatural intervention through angels.

Do Angels Give Direction?

The Bible teaches that God has given New Testament believers His Holy Spirit to lead and guide us.

Romans 8:14
For as many as are led by the Spirit of God, these are sons of God.

He has also given us His Word to be a lamp to our feet and a light to our path.

Psalm 119:105
Your word is a lamp to my feet
And a light to my path.

100

The Bible does teach that angels are used **at times** to give us guidance and direction. However, they always operate in submission to God's Word and His Spirit. In your walk with the Lord, if you ever experience an angelic appearance, always do a 'Word check', and if your spirit is trained in hearing the voice of the Holy Spirit, then also check against what the Spirit is saying. When you submit angelic ministry to these confirmations, you can be sure to avoid deception. Remember everything that is supernatural is not necessarily of God, for satan is the arch counterfeiter!

2 Corinthians 11:14
For Satan himself transforms himself into an angel of light.

More New Testament Examples of Angelic Activity

To continue with some New Testament examples of angels and their ministry, it is sobering to see what happened when King Herod did not glorify God when the people cried out in adoration after a speech he made one day. An angel was sent to execute judgment on him.

Acts 12:20-23
Now Herod had been very angry with the people of Tyre and Sidon; but they came to him with one accord, and having made Blastus the king's personal aide their friend, they asked for peace, because their

country was supplied with food by the king's country. So on a set day Herod, arrayed in royal apparel, sat on his throne and gave an oration to them. And the people kept shouting, "The voice of a god and not of a man!" Then immediately an angel of the Lord struck him, because he did not give glory to God. And he was eaten by worms and died.

In another example of angel ministry, Cornelius, an unsaved, yet devout Gentile, was visited by an angel who instructed him to send to Joppa for Peter the apostle to tell him what he needed to do (Acts 10:1-8). Peter had a vision on the rooftop of a house in Joppa while he was praying, and a voice, probably the Holy Spirit, spoke to him. When the men from Joppa arrived, the Holy Spirit did speak, giving him instructions to go with them (Acts 10:9-22). As a consequence, Peter and then the rest of the Jewish believers came to understand that God wanted them to freely preach the gospel to the Gentiles. Up to this point, they had only focused on preaching to the Jews and excluded the Gentiles. God thus used angels to bring them from one level of revelation to the next.

The church in Jerusalem was later severely persecuted under another King Herod, and Peter was thrown in prison after James the brother of John, had already been martyred. Constant prayer was offered up for Peter, and God responded by sending an angel to deliver Peter from prison. The angel gave him specific instructions and led him out of the prison. This supernatural deliverance was so dramatic that Peter only realized what was happening when he was completely free and outside the prison itself. Even the believers who were fervently praying for his deliverance found it hard to comprehend this mighty act (Acts 12:1-13).

The apostle Paul enjoyed the strengthening ministry of an angel when he was about to be shipwrecked along with over two hundred others on board ship.

Acts 27:21-25

But after long abstinence from food, then Paul stood in the midst of them and said, "Men, you should have listened to me, and not have sailed from Crete and incurred this disaster and loss. And now I urge you to take heart, for there will be no loss of life among you, but only of the ship. For there stood by me this night an angel of the God to whom I belong and whom I serve, saying, 'Do not be afraid, Paul; you must be brought before Caesar; and indeed God has granted you all those who sail with you.' Therefore take heart, men, for I believe God that it will be just as it was told me.

Paul knew to whom he belonged, and whom he served! These two key ingredients are conducive to enjoying angelic support. You must know who you belong to and who you serve. Paul was reassured that his ministry was not over, and also that God would deliver him. As a bonus, the other passengers, sailors and soldiers were all saved from a watery grave: all because of one man's complete and faithful service. I believe that our obedience and faithful lifestyle will invoke angelic help, protection and strength in our modern times too.

An angel gave the very significant 'revelation' to the exiled apostle John on the isle of Patmos close to the end of the first century.

Revelation 1:1-2
The Revelation of Jesus Christ, which God gave Him to show His servants—things which must shortly take place. And He sent and signified it by His angel to His servant John, who bore witness to the word of God, and to the testimony of Jesus Christ, to all things that he saw.

This revelation came to a man who could not be martyred like the rest of the twelve apostles. Church history records that John's persecutors tried to kill him, but could not. It appears as if God's love ran its full course in John's life. It never failed, and kept him from an early death.

Modern Examples

There are many people who testify today in our modern time to God's supernatural intervention in their lives. Testimonies of salvation and deliverance from sin, sickness and demon oppression and possession have been recorded around the world. But there are also testimonies of angelic intervention and encounters from recent Middle East wars involving Israel and her adversaries; and even from the First and Second World Wars. Soldiers in the two Gulf Wars of recent history have also reported situations where they escaped certain death, attributing their deliverance to angelic intervention. God gets the glory for sending angels to deliver them from danger.

Then, there are other personal testimonies of God's supernatural provision and deliverance that can only be attributed to angels.

In my own family, there was an incident on a Southern California three lane freeway where my wife lost control of her vehicle as she was entering from an on ramp slipway. The heavy traffic would not let her into the lane and her car veered to the right, then back onto the freeway swinging right around to face the wrong way in the middle lane of oncoming traffic that was rushing towards her. If you know anything about the traffic in California, you will appreciate her predicament. As she looked up, still facing the wrong way, there was a large semi truck and trailer bearing down on her, only yards away. She saw the whites of the eyes of the terrified driver staring at her from close range, so she closed her eyes and said to herself, 'this is it Lord'! She waited for the impact, but to her amazement there was no impact. The truck and every other vehicle barreling down the freeway at approximately sixty miles an hour plus completely missed her and came to a stop further down the freeway. She was so stirred by the incident she swung the car around and continued past all the stopped vehicles on her way. The angels assigned to her had miraculously delivered her! There is no other explanation as there was no time for the truck or the other vehicles alongside and behind it to swerve out of the way to get past her. I am convinced that her time had not yet come and God had more for her to complete in His plan.

A friend of ours was ministering in a northern Scandinavian country in wintertime. He was staying with friends in some town and decided to go for a walk out in the snow. Well, he got horribly lost, with no clue as to how to get back to the house. Everything was covered in snow, and no one dared to be out and about on foot. Suddenly there was someone who joined him and led him back to the house. This 'person' then promptly disappeared. An angel had helped him!

Are There Guardian Angels?

According to the Bible there are guardian angels assigned to each person. Jesus referred to them when He spoke of little children and 'their angels' (plural). It appears as if at least two angels are assigned to every human being as guardian angels.

> Matthew 18:10
> "Take heed that you do not despise one of these little ones, for I say to you that in heaven their angels always see the face of My Father who is in heaven.

God loves all people and has assigned angels to keep or protect us in all their ways. It is up to us to encourage their ministry in our lives by how we live for God.

How To Encourage Angelic Intervention

This may seem radical for you, but the Bible is a radical book that reveals a radical God whose love, provision and protection is available to us. I believe we have yet to see the Body of Christ fully enjoy the abundance of God's covenant grace. Simply be open to explore more of God's fullness for you. God has made an abundance of grace available to us in Christ, so why would anyone limit this grace by adopting a negative mindset towards angelic intervention and assistance. Jesus has paved the way for all our needs to be met. He has already paid the ultimate price for any provision or protection we could ever require.

The Bible teaches that certain spiritual attitudes and postures must be adopted if we are to enjoy the ministry of angels. These get God's attention, so that He might dispatch or commission His angels to minister for and on behalf of the saints. It is not so much that we command and commission angels. When we meet the conditions and cry out to God, He dispatches angels who hearken to His command.

Job 22:26-28

For then you will have your delight in the Almighty,
And lift up your face to God.
You will make your prayer to Him,
He will hear you,
And you will pay your vows.
You will also declare a thing,
And it will be established for you;
So light will shine on your ways.

When our hearts are right, bring His promises before Him in prayer, and boldly declare His will, we can expect His light to shine in our ways. We can even expect angelic intervention on our behalf.

Daniel 9:20-23

Now while I was speaking, praying, and confessing my sin and the sin of my people Israel, and presenting my supplication before the LORD my God for the holy mountain of my God, yes, while I was speaking in prayer, the man Gabriel, whom I had seen in the vision at the beginning, being caused to fly swiftly, reached me about the time of the evening offering. And he informed me, and talked with me, and said, "O Daniel, I have now come forth to give you skill to understand. At the beginning of your supplications the command went out, and I have come to tell you, for you are greatly beloved; ...

We see in this instance God giving the command to the angel in response to Daniel's prayers, supplications and confessions. Later, another angel came in response to Daniel's words!

Daniel 10:12

Then he said to me, "Do not fear, Daniel, for from the first day that you set your heart to understand, and to humble yourself before your God, your words were heard; and I have come because of your words.

Today, as you speak the Word over your finances, circumstances, health and family, angels are dispatched on your behalf. Like Daniel, be sure to stand your ground in faith. Through faith and patience, you will inherit God's promised provision and protection.

Nothing is too difficult for God. We saw earlier how Peter enjoyed miraculous deliverance from prison by means of angelic ministry.

Acts 12:5, 7

Peter was therefore kept in prison, but constant prayer was offered to God for him by the church....

...Now behold, an angel of the Lord stood by him, and a light shone in the prison; and he struck Peter on the side and raised him up, saying, "Arise quickly!" And his chains fell off his hands.

Be constant in prayer and walk in the reverential fear of the Lord. It invokes angelic protection.

Psalm 34:7

The angel of the LORD encamps all around those who fear Him, And delivers them.

When any believer chooses to make the Lord His refuge and dwell in His presence through prayer and worship, God has promised to give His angels charge over them.

Psalm 91:9-12

Because you have made the LORD, who is my refuge,

Even the Most High, your dwelling place,

No evil shall befall you,

Nor shall any plague come near your dwelling;

For He shall give His angels charge over you,

To keep you in all your ways.

In their hands they shall bear you up,

Lest you dash your foot against a stone.

When you hunger to know God and His ways, approach Him in determined prayer, worship and fasting, boldly declare His promises over your life, and walk in the fear of the Lord, you can expect angelic ministry to and for you.

Another comforting ministry of the angels is that they attend to the righteous who have died and need an escort into God's presence. The Lord Jesus spoke of angels carrying the beggar Lazarus' spirit into Abraham's bosom.

Luke 16:22

So it was that the beggar died, and was carried by the angels to Abraham's bosom...

How To Relate To God's Angels

We are not to worship them. Respect is proper, but not worship. Worship is reserved for God alone.

Revelation 22:8-9

Now I, John, saw and heard these things. And when I heard and saw, I fell down to worship before the feet of the angel who showed me these things. Then he said to me, "See that you do not do that. For I am your fellow servant, and of your brethren the prophets, and of those who keep the words of this book. Worship God."

Angels are 'fellow servants' of God, so we must reserve our worship for God alone.

Be prepared to entertain strangers: they may be angels (Hebrews 13:1). Then, be careful not to heed false doctrine taught by an angel (Galatians 1:8). Sadly, there is one major world religion and at least two modern cults with worldwide influence whose origins can be found in false doctrine taught to their founders by false, deceiving angels or demons.

When the Lord sent His angel to Moses and the children of Israel, He instructed them to be sure not to provoke Him through disobedience. When we speak and do wrong, we are sternly warned!

Exodus 23:20-22

"Behold, I send an Angel before you to keep you in the way and to bring you into the place which I have prepared. Beware of Him and obey His voice; do not provoke Him, for He will not pardon your trans-gressions; for My name is in Him. But if you indeed obey His voice and do all that I speak, then I will be an enemy to your enemies and an adversary to your adversaries.

We are not to pray to angels. The Bible teaches that all prayer is to be directed to 'the Father in Jesus name', but never to angels or any other being including our ancestors or even other godly people or saints from the past.

John 16:23
And in that day you will ask Me nothing. Most assuredly, I say to you, whatever you ask the Father in My name He will give you.

As we have seen, we can talk to angels if and when they appear, but all prayer and worship must be directed to the Father in Jesus name. Check everything you see and hear against the Word. The question is always: does it conflict with God's person, nature and will that is already revealed in His Word or not?

Is Everything Supernatural Necessarily Of God?

2 Corinthians 11:14
…For Satan himself transforms himself into an angel of light.

Satan's original name was Lucifer or 'light bearer'. He knows about light and even though he is now darkness personified, he has the ability to 'transform' himself into an angel of false 'light' to deceive ignorant and disobedient people who open themselves up to his influence and sometimes even possession.

Unfortunately, he can exploit man's hunger for the supernatural. Most people live out their lives not experiencing much of the supernatural at all. When something supernatural happens, it gets their attention. But if they are not careful and schooled in God's Word, their curiosity can lead them astray. You cannot assume just because you have had some supernatural experience that it is automatically from God. Supernatural experiences must be judged in the light of the Word and not the other way round.

This is critical as many people have gone astray basing their lives on what they thought to be from God simply because it was supernatural. Supernatural experiences must line up with God's Word. I know of people who have been shipwrecked in their faith, because they refuse to acknowledge that their supernatural experience was not of God, even when the scripture was clear about the matter at hand.

Conclusion

God's angels are our friends, sent by God to minister to and for the people of God. As you walk closely with the Lord and obey His Word, your faith and obedience opens the door to angelic ministry. Do not shut off this aspect of God's overall plan through doubt and unbelief. Angels are an integral part of God's provision and protection to further His purposes in these exciting end times.

Angels Summary Fact Sheet

• Definition – 'messengers' / 'ministers' of God.
Luke 2:9-15

• Created at one point in time and do not propagate.
Psalm 148:3-5 / Colossians 1:16

• Main abode – heaven, but also sent to earth.
Matthew 22:30

• Their nature – spirit beings that can appear bodily.
Psalm 104:4

• Possess some wisdom, but are not all wise like God.
2 Samuel 14:20 / 1 Peter 1:12

• Exercise great strength.
Isaiah 37:6 / Psalm 103:20 / Matthew 28:2 / Acts 5:19

• Under Christ's authority.
1 Peter 3:22

• Number – 'innumerable company' or millions.
Jeremiah 33:22a / Hebrews 12:22

• Classified and ranked: orderly & under command.
1 Peter 3:22 / Ephesians 1:21

• Prayer to the Father activates angelic ministry.
Matthew 26:53 / Daniel 10:1-21

• They 'hearken to' or give attention to and obey the voice of God's word.
Psalm 103:20

• They minister to and for God.
Revelation 7:11 / Acts 12:23

• They minister to and for Jesus.
Matthew 4:11 / Matthew 13:41

• They minister to and for the saints (believers.)
Daniel 10:18-19 / Acts 12:7-11

• They are not to be confused with satan who can pose as an 'angel of light'.
2 Corinthians 11:14

Satan does not have any 'creative' ability. He does not originate anything, but rather pollutes, frustrates and opposes the God given life, passions and needs of mankind that are already in place.

Chapter 6

Know Your Enemies

Introduction

2 Corinthians 2:11

…lest Satan should take advantage of us; for we are
not ignorant of his devices.

I can remember as a newly born again Christian not wanting
to know anything about the devil and demons. I was even
somewhat frightened by the pictures on the covers of some
of the Bible teaching books on the subject. Later, I came to
realize that God wanted me to know how the devil operated.
My reluctance and fear was a trick of the enemy to keep me
ignorant of him. In this environment of spiritual ignorance
and darkness, he could continue to work undetected. Sadly I
believe many Christians are harassed by the enemy without
knowing what to do, simply because they are ignorant of his

devices. I encourage you to read on and find out the authority you have over satan and demons, especially when you know they have already been defeated by the Lord Jesus Christ. It is not that you will become so devil conscious that you lose your focus on God. Rather you will know just enough about your enemy and his tactics to enforce his defeat every time. All good warriors know their enemy.

To be forewarned is forearmed!

The Devil Is Real

The devil and demons are not the product of unbalanced minds, steeped in superstition and ignorance as some so called educated persons would have you believe. They are very real spirit beings that even the Lord Jesus Christ spoke about. He even cast them out of people. They were real to Him, and He was not delusional, but walked in the Spirit acutely aware of their existence and spiritual influence. He even spoke to the devil at the time of His temptations in the wilderness. It would be foolish to deny the existence of the devil and demons when even Jesus is recorded as talking to them! Only the Word of God presents a proper perspective on their existence and importance. When you pay too much or too little attention to him, it is equally dangerous, for he wants either to remain hidden in the dark, or perversely to be the center of attention.

Basic Facts About Satan And Demons

Satan

Satan is a fallen angel previously named 'Lucifer', 'light bearer' or 'morning star'. He was created perfect, and was supposed to shine forth God's glory. He later became corrupted by his own pride, and iniquity was found in him, and so was cast out of God's presence.

> Isaiah 14:12-15
> "How you are fallen from heaven,
> O Lucifer, son of the morning!
> How you are cut down to the ground,
> You who weakened the nations!
> For you have said in your heart:
> 'I will ascend into heaven,
> I will exalt my throne above the stars of God;
> I will also sit on the mount of the congregation
> On the farthest sides of the north;
> I will ascend above the heights of the clouds,
> I will be like the Most High.'
> Yet you shall be brought down to Sheol,
> To the lowest depths of the Pit.

He was not created in God's image like man, and it turned out that he wanted to usurp a position that did not belong to him. As a result of his pride and selfish ambition, (represented by the five 'I wills' found in the above passage), he was brought low or humbled.

Today, he still seeks to exalt himself by influencing ungodly spiritually blinded men who yield to his lies. In the following passage, He is described as 'the king of Tyre', a double reference to an earthly king at the time, and is revealed to have been perfect in the day he was created. He was beautiful and attractive, seemingly with musical abilities (timbrels and pipes) built into him, which were to be employed in leading worship to God in heaven. However, 'iniquity was found in him' due to the success he enjoyed in trading precious goods. His heart was lifted up by this abundance, and he corrupted his own wisdom. The source of all iniquity was found in satan, and cannot be traced back to God. God did not create evil and was obliged to cast this rebellious angel called the 'anointed cherub who covers' to the ground. Rebellion is a destructive force that cannot be tolerated in God's kingdom.

Ezekiel 28:11-17

Moreover the word of the LORD came to me, saying, "Son of man, take up a lamentation for the king of Tyre, and say to him, 'Thus says the Lord GOD: "You were the seal of perfection, Full of wisdom and perfect in beauty. You were in Eden, the garden of God; Every precious stone was your covering: The sardius, topaz, and diamond, Beryl, onyx, and jasper, Sapphire, turquoise, and emerald with gold. The workmanship of your timbrels and pipes was prepared for you on the day you were created. "You were the anointed cherub who covers; I established you; You were on the holy mountain of God; You walked back and forth in the midst of fiery stones. You were perfect in your ways from the day you were created, Till iniquity was found in you. "By the abundance of your trading You became filled with violence within, And you sinned; Therefore I cast you as a profane thing Out of the mountain of God; And I destroyed you, O covering cherub, From the midst of the fiery stones. "Your heart was lifted up because of your beauty; You corrupted your wisdom for the sake of your splendor; I cast you to the ground, I laid you before kings, That they might gaze at you.

Original sin actually took place in the heart of Lucifer, and he brought this rebellion to the earth as a fallen angel, now named satan. He then tempted Adam and Eve who were God's highest order of created being and co-under rulers on the earth. In the Garden of Eden, we see satan exploit Adam and Eve's lack of clear communication. Adam's lack of conviction to protect his wife from deception, and satan's guile when he questioned the integrity of God's Word, provided the soil for him to sow doubt in Eve's heart. The 'serpent', or 'poisoner', drove a wedge between man and woman and their God. He opened up a separation in both relationships, and has employed these tactics ever since. He also introduced 'fear' as the ruling spirit the world.

Genesis 3:1-10

Now the serpent was more cunning than any beast of the field which the LORD God had made. And he said to the woman, "Has God indeed said, 'You shall not eat of every tree of the garden'?" And the woman said to the serpent, "We may eat the fruit of the trees of the garden; but of the fruit of the tree which is in the midst of the garden, God has said, 'You shall not eat it, nor shall you touch it, lest you die.'" Then the serpent said to the woman, "You will not surely die. For God knows that in the day you eat of it your eyes will be opened, and you will be like God, knowing good and evil." So when the woman saw that the tree was good for food, that it was pleasant to the eyes, and a tree desirable to make one wise, she took of its fruit and ate. She also gave to her husband with her, and he ate. Then the eyes of both of them were opened, and they knew that they were naked; and they sewed fig leaves together and made themselves coverings. And they heard the sound of the LORD God walking in the garden in the cool of the day, and Adam and his wife hid themselves from the presence of the LORD God among the trees of the garden.

Then the LORD God called to Adam and said to him, "Where are you?" So he said, "I heard Your voice in the garden, and I was afraid because I was naked; and I hid myself."

Satan is not some impersonal evil influence, but a definite spirit-being or personality that can and does strategize evil plots. He even communicates with whoever is foolish or ignorant enough to listen to his lies. Having the attributes of a personal being, he can exercise his will, enact acts attributable only to a real being, and possess faculties that allow him to be a murderer and liar. The point here is that no impersonal 'force' or 'influence' can engineer these, only a real being.

John 8:44-45

You are of your father the devil, and the desires of your father you want to do. He was a murderer from the beginning, and does not stand in the truth, because there is no truth in him. When he speaks a lie, he speaks from his own resources, for he is a liar and the father of it.

His Names And Titles Reveal His ...

Character and Operations

When you know the names given to satan, you know how he operates through deception and destruction. In the Bible he is called:

• Abbadon or Apollyon – the destroyer of good. Revelation 9:11

• Accuser – the one who brings charges against. Revelation 12:13

• Adversary – one who opposes. 1 Peter 5:8

• Angel of light – a deceiver posing as another. 2 Corinthians 11:13-15

• Beelzebub – lord or prince of the flies, later dunghill. Matthew 10:25

• Belial – good for nothing / worthless. Deuteronomy 13:13

• Devil – 'diablos' -deceiver who presents lies as truth. Revelation 12:9

• Dragon – 'sea monster' arising out of rebellious humanity. Revelation 20:2

• God of this world (age) – aspiring to religious rule. 2 Corinthians 4:4

• Lawless one – reveals his wicked and evil intent. Matthew 13:38

• Liar – and the father of all lies. John 8:44

• Prince of this world – rule and influence in world affairs. John 12:31

• Satan – the one who hinders, opposes, withstands. 1 Thessalonians 2:18

• Serpent – hisses or whispers with intent to enchant. Genesis 3:1

• Tempter – entice, try or scrutinize. Matthew 4:3

• Thief – steals that which rightfully belongs to others. John 10:10

Satan does not have any 'creative' ability either. He does not originate anything, but rather pollutes, frustrates and opposes the God given life, passions and desires of mankind that are already in place. Satan is like a virus that takes advantage of what is already there in the human body. Viruses corrupt the normal functions in the body, and are dependent on the processes already in place.

Satan is the 'arch corrupter' of all that God has made good. When God made everything, He saw that it 'was good' (Genesis 1:4, 9, 12, 17, 21, 25). In short everything that satan is and tries to do in your life, must be resisted with God's truth. Do not agree with, receive or cooperate with any of his distractions, devices or evil scheming. Satan is thus the author of all that is bad and evil. Do not buy into his lie that God is sometimes the author of evil and even works on occasion with the devil to achieve His ends.

Is There Ever A 'Good Side' To The Devil?

Absolutely not! He is a liar and the father of all lies. He would have unsuspecting people believe that he is not that bad. He is bad to the core, vicious and untrustworthy. His nature is to steal, kill and destroy (John 10:10). He cannot be good, just as God cannot be bad. Some claim to do 'white witchcraft' for the benefit of mankind. All witchcraft is an abomination to God and does no one any good at any time (Deuteronomy 18:10-12). The so called 'healings' performed in satan's name, always lead to some other deeper bondage later on. Involvement in any form of witchcraft opens the door for satan to access more of a person's life and habits.

Satan is a deceiver and always intent on man's destruction. His nature determines his mode of operation.

John 10:10
The thief does not come except to steal, and to kill, and to destroy. I have come that they may have life, and that they may have it more abundantly.

In contrast to the gift of life that Jesus comes to give us, satan only comes to take what does not belong to him. He is a thief by nature, totally fallen and depraved. Like the proverbial snake that hitched a ride across the river on the turtle's back, and then bit his neck half way across, after promising not to, satan cannot help but be evil and untrustworthy. It is in his nature to lie and deceive. His names reveal his nature and how he operates to spoil mankind as the pinnacle of God's creation. Man is the only creature created in the exact likeness of God, and satan is insanely jealous of man's position in God. He is illegally trying to use mankind to usurp authority in the spirit.

Evil Spirits Or Demons

A demon is an inferior spirit of an evil nature that 'distributes' evil on the earth. Jesus recognized their personal existence, addressing them whilst He exercised authority over them.

Matthew 8:28-32

When He had come to the other side, to the country of the Gergesenes, there met Him two demon-possessed men, coming out of the tombs, exceedingly fierce, so that no one could pass that way. And suddenly they cried out, saying, "What have we to do with You, Jesus, You Son of God? Have You come here to torment us before the time?" Now a good way off from them there was a herd of many swine feeding. So the demons begged Him, saying, "If You cast us out, permit us to go away into the herd of swine." And He said to them, "Go." So when they had come out, they went into the herd of swine. And suddenly the whole herd of swine ran violently down the steep place into the sea, and perished in the water.

Two demon-possessed men met Jesus that day, and the demons spoke through the men. Jesus recognized their personal existence and spoke back to them in the process of casting them out. Some people doubt the existence of demons, relying on their limited reasoning powers to try to explain away evil practices. Yet Jesus recognized their existence. It is a trick of the enemy to get well meaning yet ignorant Christians to avoid dealing with demons by doubting whether they exist or not, or being fearful of them.

Where Do Demons Come From?

There are three main views as to where demons come from. First, some claim that demons are fallen angels who fell along with satan (Lucifer) according to Isaiah 14:12 and Matthew 25:41. There are two classes: those bound in 'Tartarus' (hell) and in the 'abyss'; and others that are not. These operate under satan's command as 'demons' in both the earth and the second heaven or atmosphere, and exist according to rank. The devil's kingdom thus functions in counterfeit of God's faithful angels.

Second, some argue that demons are disembodied spirits of some supposed pre – Adamic race of beings according to the description found in Genesis 1:1-2. The earth was formless and void because of a supposed chaotic satanic disturbance before Adam and Eve were placed on the earth. The earth had to be 'recreated' at this time, so the argument goes, because God does not make anything 'formless and void' to start with. The 'recreation' is supposed to start with verse three in Genesis Chapter One.

A third view maintains that demons are the offspring of angels cohabiting with pre – flood women according to Genesis 6:1-4.

Rather than debate and get hung up at this point over each argument, it is best to focus on the fact that demons simply do exist, and more importantly, that Jesus has broken their power, and commissioned us to cast them out whenever we come across them.

Mark 16:15-17

"… Go into all the world and preach the gospel to every creature. He who believes and is baptized will be saved; but he who does not believe will be condemned. And these signs will follow those who believe: In My name they will cast out demons; they will speak with new tongues; …

It is my view that it is best to focus on the authority **we** now have over these demon spirits, and not on their origin.

What Are Demons Like?

The Bible teaches that demons are evil, morally corrupt spirit beings who reflect the nature and character of their diabolical leader satan. They have names (Luke 8:30), a capacity to make choices and to speak (Luke 4:33-35), and have limited knowledge of spiritual matters (Mark 1:21-24). They do not know all things about you. Only God knows everything about you.

When people yield to demons and become possessed, the demons can be of tremendous strength (Acts 19:14-16). The sons of Sceva found that out when they tried to cast out a demon, without Jesus backing them with His authority and power. Some demons are more wicked than others, according to Matthew 12:45 and they can become 'familiar' with people especially when they give them access through disobedience and occult dabbling (fortune telling, tarot cards, horoscopes, Ouija boards etc). These 'familiar' spirits can know some things about people, and reveal these supernaturally to unsuspecting so called 'ministers' who very often are not even aware that the devil is using them (Leviticus 20:6,27).

Satan uses demons to extend his influence, because, unlike God, he is **not** omnipresent. He is limited and has to move from place to place, as do his demons. He uses various ranks of demons to hinder the 'saints' according to Ephesians 6:12, and 1 Thessalonians 2:18. Demons draw people away from the faith (2 Timothy 4:1), and encourage idolatrous practices around the world (1 Corinthians 10:19-21). They can even cause physical afflictions as Luke 13:11-6 and Acts 10:38 record.

The Devil And Demons Are Already Defeated!

Many fearful people are captivated by satan's lies and deception. He would have them believe he is almost as big and powerful as God. Thankfully, God's Word is the final authority on this. See the devil from God's perspective. **Only God** is all powerful. When the Lord rose from the dead He was victorious over the devil and all his demons. He stripped them of all their authority, totally defeating them at His resurrection. In short, they are defeated foes.

Colossians 2:15
Having disarmed principalities and powers, He made a public spectacle of them, triumphing over them in it.

This total defeat is to be **'enforced'** by the triumphant church. So in essence, we are not fighting to gain a victory, but fighting **from** a victory already won almost two thousand years ago. We must consider ourselves more of an occupying army, than a conquering one. We hold to a **position already established** by Christ's victory. The land has been given to us. It is ours, and **satan must be evicted** from territory he illegally holds on to!

God is therefore not hoping to defeat the devil, nor is He struggling with him. The battle is already won, and our instructions are to go make disciples of the nations, preach the gospel to every creature and cast out any devil that gets in the way as we go. Really, we are involved in a 'mopping up' operation!

Matthew 28:18-19
"All authority has been given to Me in heaven and on earth. Go therefore and make disciples of all the nations, ...

Also, the record shows that Jesus saw satan 'fall like lightning' from heaven, so we know that satan's character is fatally flawed and doomed to final destruction. He is fallen, and cannot get up!

Luke 10:17-18
Then the seventy returned with joy, saying, "Lord, even the demons are subject to us in Your name." And He said to them, "I saw Satan fall like lightning from heaven.

A future, eternal judgment awaits him, so with all this in mind, why fear him in any way?

Revelation 20:10
The devil, who deceived them, was cast into the lake of fire and brimstone where the beast and the false prophet are. And they will be tormented day and night forever and ever.

Why Then, Do Some Christians Still Struggle With The Enemy?

Ephesians 4:27
... nor give place to the devil.

As a believer in the Lord Jesus Christ, you are under His lordship, and no longer a child of the devil. Satan does not have 'unlimited' access to you, except where he finds a 'place' that he has been given to do his dirty work.

There are some key reasons why some Christians still have a hard time with the enemy. I am not talking about persecution for righteousness sake here. Satan will oppose God's people in whatever way he can, regardless of whether they give him place to move or not. Rather, these are areas where we have a part to play in giving him access to things that should be under our control. In this section you will learn how to **close the door** to the enemy's operation.

First, he will exploit any **ignorance** of what belongs to you in Christ.

Hosea 4:6

My people are destroyed for lack of knowledge...

When the saints are ignorant of their covenant rights privileges and responsibilities, and there are many, satan takes advantage of this and does his dirty work in that spiritual 'darkness'. I know of many Christians who simply put up with far too much grief from the devil without exercising their God – given authority to bind his operations. Gullibility is a function of ignorance, and any occult or hidden activity takes place where God's light does not shine. God's word is a lamp and a light, and serves to expose what satan is doing. Where His light (His Word) is not known or understood, satan has a field day, and is free to do his dirty deceptive work.

There are whole denominations of Christendom that suffer unnecessary bondage to sickness and poverty due to ignorance of what Christ has provided for them through His promises. For example, if you do not know that God wants you and your family to prosper and have all your needs met, and how to access God's blessings through tithing, offerings and faithful participation in your local church, you will suffer unnecessary financial hardship.

3 John 2
Beloved, I pray that you may prosper in all things and be in health, just as your soul prospers.

This truth applies also in the areas of health and soul prosperity (mental / emotional realm). When you know God's promises of total well being, healing and health, you can stand against sickness, disease and distress in your life. If you do not, you allow satan room to move in this area and bring sickness and distress upon you.

Second, a simple **lack of resistance** to his maneuvers will give him a place of access. We are instructed in God's Word to resist the devil, not simply roll over and 'play dead' hoping that he will move on to someone else. No, he is ruthless and malicious, and will take advantage of any passivity. You have to stand your ground and fight him off with the word! You resist him when you boldly declare your covenant with the faith confessions of your mouth. Of course your lifestyle must match your mouth.

James 4:7

Therefore submit to God. Resist the devil and he will flee from you.

Two things must happen before the devil flees from you. First, you have to submit to God, that is, His Word. Second, you have to use that Word against the devil. Wield your sword! Pick it up and use it by speaking the promises of God over any situation you are facing. Keep on doing this till you get the victory. Satan cannot tolerate the light of the spoken word coming out of the mouth of believers who are standing their ground in faith! For example, if you face a financial lack, pay your tithes, give an offering into God's work and boldly declare that God will supply your every need according to His riches. Watch things turn around as you stand in faith and patience for the season to produce.

Let us look at a third area that satan exploits.

An **ill-disciplined thought life** opens up the door to your adversary. God expects us to think right, because if we do not, we will move in the direction of those bad thoughts. God expects us to bring any wayward thoughts into captivity. In this way, we will not allow satan to build up fortresses or 'strongholds' of incorrect thinking that block God's will for our lives. We saw in an earlier chapter that the mind is the arena of spiritual warfare. When we 'pull down' arguments and high things in our minds that oppose or exalt themselves against the knowledge of God, we do damage to satan's operation in our lives. He wants our thinking to be all messed up and prideful, because he knows that God will not have his way in this confusion. When we think straight, we will obey, and all disobedience is thus punished. Replace negative thoughts with positive ones from God's Word. You have the power to choose to think positively. It is very possible and we are commanded by God to do just that. Practice thinking positively. It is not an empty exercise but a Biblical one.

Philippians 4:8
Finally, brethren, whatever things are true, whatever things are noble, whatever things are just, whatever things are pure, whatever things are lovely, whatever things are of good report, if there is any virtue and if there is anything praiseworthy — meditate on these things.

Fourth, a prideful **refusal to humble oneself** before the Lord's Table, opens the door to the enemy. God expects us to judge ourselves in the light of His Word and make any changes of heart or practice that will close the door to adversity.

1 Corinthians 11:29-32

For he who eats and drinks in an unworthy manner eats and drinks judgment to himself, not discerning the Lord's body. For this reason many are weak and sick among you, and many sleep. For if we would judge ourselves, we would not be judged. But when we are judged, we are chastened by the Lord, that we may not be condemned with the world.

Here, some Corinthian church members got sick and died an early death because they did not humble themselves and judge the wrongs in their lives. They continued to partake of communion in an unworthy manner, and thus brought judgment on themselves. The enemy found a place to exploit, and they suffered the consequences. Communion is supposed to be one of the ways in which the Lord keeps His people healthy, yet satan was taking advantage of their carnality! Close the door to satan's operations by living a self examined holy life. Here it is not so much looking at our hearts as it is seeing where we have not yet partaken of the benefits of Jesus completed work. Christians struggle in areas where they have little or no revelation of God's goodness and love towards them. We live holy because He is holy and lives in us. God's grace or divine favor and enablement causes us to walk in the light of His victory. We access His grace to live right and in authority over satan by the faith God gives us as His gift.

Another area satan gains access is through the **friends you keep company with.** Friends will either help you or hinder you in your walk with the Lord.

Proverbs 12:26
The righteous should choose his friends carefully,
For the way of the wicked leads them astray.

What are friends for? They are to help keep you on track with God. A friend, who is wicked, is not a true friend. Close the door to your adversary by cultivating godly friendships. This does not mean you cannot pray for and witness to old friends, but do not 'hang out' with them. Let what you have rub off on them, rather than the reverse.

Another way in which satan takes advantage of us is simply through being slack in our approach to life and work. Yes that is right; slothfulness is a sixth tool of the enemy.

Proverbs 18:9
He who is slothful in his work
Is a brother to him who is a great destroyer.

Lack of discipline and a poor work ethic will work against you. Slothfulness is in the same family as brother 'destruction', and this kind is not a good brother to have. Once again, make the choice to obey God, work hard and honestly, and watch God reward your faithfulness and integrity. Close the door to the 'destroyer' as you get up from the couch and switch the TV off. In all labor there is profit. Time is God's gift to us, so use it wisely.

Proverbs 14:23
In all labor there is profit,
But idle chatter leads only to poverty.

In short, you can close the door to the enemy by:

• Knowing Who Christ is in you – the Greater One

• Knowing what belongs to you in Christ

• Actively resisting satan with your mouth

• Watching over your thought life

• Leading a self examined life at communion

• Keeping company with godly friends

• Living a disciplined, productive godly life.

The 'Levels' Of Demonic Influence

There are different levels of demonic influence in people's lives. We all live in a fallen world and are subject to temptation. Even Jesus was tempted to do wrong, and He was perfect! Satan can gain increasing influence in a person's life over time if they let him! As we have seen, he does not have unlimited access to our lives. However, if no stand is made against his lies and deceit in the mental realm, he will begin increasingly to seek control through temptation, depression, oppression and finally full possession where a person's will is taken over by evil spirits.

Up to this point, satan's focus is on influencing the flesh and the unrenewed mind of man, but as he gains more and more access, he goes after controlling the spirit of a man. The spirit is the core of our being that satan ultimately wants to control. The tactics he uses to gain control of our lives include **devaluing** God's Word, **distracting** and **diverting** us from the things of God, and **discouragement** when things do not work out quickly enough in the way we expected. **Despair** can set in, and deception quickly follows where some falsehood is substituted for the truth. This lie then begins to dominate our thoughts, emotions and actions to the point where satan is in control.

Guard against even the slightest demonic influence. Small cracks will widen in time if the door is not shut to the devil. Keep the door firmly shut by staying as close to God and as far from the devil as you know how.

Isaiah 54:14

In righteousness you shall be established;

You shall be far from oppression, for you shall not fear;
And from terror, for it shall not come near you.

How To Deal With Fear Or Intimidation

When Adam sinned, satan was able to introduce a ruling spirit of fear into the earth (Genesis 3:10). Up till this time, mankind did not know any fear at all. But as Adam fell from the heights at which God had placed him, he experienced fear for the first time. Since that time, fear has been the ruling expression of satan's influence, and men have been paralyzed by fear and intimidation. Even today in the end-times, Jesus prophesied that men's hearts would be 'failing them from fear, and the expectation of those things which are coming on the earth for the powers of heaven will be shaken' (Luke 21:26). Satan's goal has always been to immobilize God's people from boldly speaking God's Word over their own lives. Fear is the force that attracts evil, just as faith attracts good. God has shown us in His Word that we no longer have a 'spirit of fear' ruling us. Now that we are born again we have been given a new spirit of 'power, love and a sound mind'. It is a feature of the new creation.

2 Timothy 1:7
For God has not given us a spirit of fear, but of power and of love and of a sound mind.

The first step in walking free from fear is to recognize that fear is no longer your master. The second step is to pray for the boldness needed to continue speaking God's Word in the face of opposition. Even the great apostle Paul asked for prayer help in this regard, and we should too.

Ephesians 6:18-19

... praying always with all prayer and supplication in the Spirit, being watchful to this end with all perseverance and supplication for all the saints— and for me, that utterance may be given to me, that I may open my mouth boldly to make known the mystery of the gospel, ...

The early disciples also needed prayer support when under demonic attack from the persecuting authorities of the day.

Acts 4:23-29

And being let go, they went to their own companions and reported all that the chief priests and elders had said to them. So when they heard that, they raised their voice to God with one accord and said: "Lord, You are God, who made heaven and earth and the sea, and all that is in them, who by the mouth of Your servant David have said: 'Why did the nations rage, And the people plot vain things?

The kings of the earth took their stand,
And the rulers were gathered together
Against the LORD and against His Christ.'
"For truly against Your holy Servant Jesus, whom You anointed, both Herod and Pontius Pilate, with the Gentiles and the people of Israel, were gathered together to do whatever Your hand and Your purpose determined before to be done. Now, Lord, look on their threats, and grant to Your servants that with all boldness they may speak Your word,

They turned their attention to prayer to God when they were threatened and felt intimidated. They did not shift their focus onto the devil and try to 'war against' him in some weird way. They cried out to God for boldness to continue what He had commissioned them to do. In like manner, solicit prayer support when you feel fearful, and keep your eyes on Jesus.

How The Accuser Brings Charges Against God's People

Revelation 12:10
Then I heard a loud voice saying in heaven, "Now salvation, and strength, and the kingdom of our God, and the power of His Christ have come, for the accuser of our brethren, who accused them before our God day and night, has been cast down.

Satan is described as the 'accuser of the brethren'. He will exploit an element of 'truth' in your life that shows some hypocrisy, insincerity, selfish motives, or even a secret vice. His tactic is to then 'accuse' or heap condemnation on you, tempting you to feel hopeless about the area of your life that has not yet come under Christ's Lordship.

In contrast to the devil's accusations, when God deals with you about some area that needs to change, He will convict or convince you of the need and value of making the necessary change. As the God of hope, He will impart His hope **and** the grace you need through His Word so that you can overcome the problem.

When you despair and begin to doubt, know that the devil is at work. To shut him up, revisit in the Word what God says about you as a new creation. You are saved by grace through faith in His completed work on the cross, not by your own works or attempts at achieving perfection. God knows that you have to grow up in your new position of righteousness in Christ, and that this process takes time. Like any child learning to live in the world has loving parents teaching them how to stay out of trouble, your Heavenly Father will not give up on you when you stumble. Neither will He condemn you for messing up. He has already forgiven you, and wants you to be secure in His everlasting love for you so that you can keep on going forward in faith and confidence.

Acknowledge your sin to God, but thank Him that His blood has already cleansed you from that sin. The next time the 'accuser' tries to drag you down, tell him you are the righteousness of God in Christ (2 Corinthians 5:21), and that you and he have parted company forever. Jesus is now your Lord, and you are only listening to His voice now!

How Jesus Engaged In Spiritual Warfare

Jesus faced intense opposition wherever He went. He was constantly at odds with the devil and demons, yet we have no record of Him engaging in some suspect spiritual warfare practice. He was successful over the works of the devil because He was secure in His sonship and was anointed by the Holy Spirit to fulfill His destiny.

Acts 10:38
…how God anointed Jesus of Nazareth with the Holy Spirit and with power, who went about doing good and healing all who were oppressed by the devil, for God was with Him.

God was with Him in the same way that the Holy Spirit is with us. In the heat of battle God will neither leave nor forsake you (Hebrews 13:5 / Isaiah 41:10).

God had prepared Jesus for over 30 years, filling Him with the Word according to Luke 2:52. Jesus had also waited for His heavenly Father's perfect timing, being baptized by John where the heavens were opened to Him. God declared that he was well pleased with Jesus as His 'beloved son' before Jesus had done anything in His new ministry for His Father in heaven. In like manner we should learn to minister out of a position of secure sonship. Later Jesus successfully resisted the devil's temptations in the wilderness by speaking the Word. Jesus ran him off by quoting relevant scripture (Matthew 4:1-11) that contradicted the temptations. He thus set the platform for successful ministry, and begun to fulfill His purpose to destroy the works of the devil through teaching, preaching and healing the sick (1 John 3:8 / Matthew 4:23-24).

He initially enjoyed considerable success wherever He went and was well received. Although He later faced strong opposition, betrayal and apparent defeat on the cross, we know that it was all in God's plan, and the tables were ultimately turned on satan. When Jesus rose victorious over death, hell and the grave, He **disarmed** satan of **all** authority on earth and under the earth (Colossians 2:15). He ascended to the highest position and made it possible for God to seat **us** in Christ at His right hand (Ephesians 2:5).

Nowhere do we see Jesus 'pulling down' strongholds over Jerusalem or any other city or region. He simply prayed, obeyed and went about teaching preaching, healing and casting out devils.

Matthew 4:23-25
And Jesus went about all Galilee, teaching in their synagogues, preaching the gospel of the kingdom, and

healing all kinds of sickness and all kinds of disease among the people. Then His fame went throughout all Syria; and they brought to Him all sick people who were afflicted with various diseases and torments, and those who were demon-possessed, epileptics, and paralytics; and He healed them. Great multitudes followed Him—from Galilee, and from Decapolis, Jerusalem, Judea, and beyond the Jordan.

He operated under an anointing that had come to rest upon Him at His baptism. The heavens had been opened to Him at the Jordan River, and from that moment on He walked under an open heaven (Matthew 3:16). His connection with His Heavenly Father was unhindered, and He was able to exercise all authority over His adversary the devil. He ministered with authority and power because He was submitted to God. Thank God for the wonderful example Jesus gives us. When we submit to God and go in Jesus name, we do not have to resort to dubious spiritual warfare practices.

Of course satan did not want to let go of his control, and would oppose Jesus authority in whatever way he could. Yet time and again he was cast out with a word, and defeated.

When Jesus faced His own personal spiritual struggles, He faced them with faith, and willingly consecrated Himself to do God's will no matter the cost. In the Garden of Gethsemane just before Jesus was betrayed, He engaged in a tremendous prayer battle. He fought it alone, as His disciples had fallen asleep in the heat of the moment. Yet God sustained Him in this time of extraordinary trial. This incident shows us where the battle truly lies: between the flesh and the spirit. Satan was attempting to get at Jesus through His flesh.

> Matthew 26:39-41
>
> He went a little farther and fell on His face, and prayed, saying, "O My Father, if it is possible, let this cup pass from Me; nevertheless, not as I will, but as You will." Then He came to the disciples and found them asleep, and said to Peter, "What? Could you not watch with Me one hour? Watch and pray, lest you enter into temptation. The spirit indeed is willing, but the flesh is weak."

Spiritual warfare has more to with bringing the flesh under the dominion of God, than 'squaring off' with the devil. When we follow Jesus' example and consecrate in faith to live for God no matter what, the devil will have no room to move and fail in his attempts to discourage us.

How The Apostles Waged Spiritual Warfare

Jesus extended His authority to His disciples by delegating to them authority over demons and disease. They went out under His command and exercised this authority without practicing any odd spiritual warfare practices.

Luke 9:1-2, 6

Then He called His twelve disciples together and gave them power and authority over all demons, and to cure diseases. He sent them to preach the kingdom of God and to heal the sick…So they departed and went through the towns, preaching the gospel and healing everywhere.

The apostles and early Christians were well able to fulfill the commission God gave them to reach their generation despite intense opposition, persecution and lack of modern communication and travel resources. The people groups or nations they ministered to were most often riddled with idol (demon) worship, yet they were able to overcome all sorts of opposition.

As we have seen, in the early days of the church in Jerusalem, the apostle Peter and the whole company of believers resorted to prayer when faced with severe persecution from the ruling elders and scribes who were threatened by their growth (Acts 4:23-31). Nowhere in their prayers or actions do you see the believers 'warring' in tongues against the 'ruling spirit of religious Judaism' in Jerusalem. Rather, they asked God for continued boldness to speak the Word, and that signs and wonders would confirm their ministry. This ought to be a central focus of our spiritual warfare too: boldness in the face of opposition and miracles.

Again later, when Peter was imprisoned by King Herod for His faith (Acts 12:5), 'constant prayer' was offered by the saints for his deliverance. God hearkened to their words, commissioning angels to go release him from prison. Supernaturally, he was delivered back to the astonished but still praying company of believers. Once again in this dramatic spiritual warfare example, the prayer focus was on God, not on the devil and demons. All prayer should focus on God's person and promises, but never on the devil.

Even Paul and Silas did not war against the devil as they sat chained in a stinking Philippian prison, persecuted for their obedience. Rather they prayed and sang hymns to God in that desperate darkness. After being thrown in jail for ministering to a slave girl possessed with a spirit of divination, they never focused on the devil, nor tried to pull down some 'stronghold of divination' in the city. The spirit had already been cast out! They kept their eyes on God who responded to their faith by supernaturally delivering them when the earthquake shook the region. Their chains fell off, and they were set free to continue ministering in God's power (Acts 16:16-26).

In another example of spiritual warfare when Paul ministered in Athens, Greece, he confronted the gross Athenian idolatry with a bold preaching of the Word (Acts 17:16-17).

Acts 17:16-17

16 Now while Paul waited for them at Athens, his spirit was provoked within him when he saw that the city was given over to idols. 17 Therefore he reasoned in the synagogue with the Jews and with the Gentile worshipers, and in the marketplace daily with those who happened to be there.

Neither he, nor his fellow travelers warred against the ruling 'idol spirits' of that influential city. He simply proclaimed the gospel which had and always will have the power to save. The gospel or good news is God's power to salvation (Romans 1:16). Good news always trumps bad news.

When he preached in the Ephesian synagogues, and then after three months in their local 'school of Tyrannus' he paid no attention to the 'ruling Diana spirit' of the city, but continued to faithfully preach the gospel. He was so successful in this, that in the space of two years, all of Asia Minor, (Turkey as it is known today), heard the gospel go out from that influential regional gateway port city.

Acts 19:8-10

And he went into the synagogue and spoke boldly for three months, reasoning and persuading concerning the things of the kingdom of God. But when some were hardened and did not believe, but spoke evil of the Way before the multitude, he departed from them and withdrew the disciples, reasoning daily in the school of Tyrannus. And this continued for two years, so that all who dwelt in Asia heard the word of the Lord Jesus, both Jews and Greeks.

The gospel must be preached for men to be saved. To lose that focus is to lose the power. Effective Word based prayer and bold anointed preaching is the core of God's plan to reach the world and successfully enforce satans' defeat. Never substitute preaching the gospel with some odd 'warfare' prayer practices.

You Have Authority Over The Devil And Demons

If Jesus cast out devils with a word (Matthew 8:16), and His Word is alive and active in your heart (John 14:12), you can use that Word to do exactly the same. In fact, Jesus said one of the signs that would follow you as you spoke the Word in His name, is that you would cast out demons (Mark 16:15-16).

You have both the permission and power in His name to cast them out. The record shows that His disciples exercised their authority over demons on several occasions both in the gospels and the book of Acts.

First, the disciples cast out devils when they went out and ministered in Jesus name according to Luke 9:1. Later, Phillip the evangelist cast out demons (Acts 8:6-7). Paul the apostle also cast out devils as recorded in Acts 16:16-18.

This was therefore quite a common practice among believers in those days, and also throughout two thousand years of church history. This practice is still common in our time through those who are taught correctly in this doctrine. Even though you may not have seen or experienced much of this sort of ministry, be open to and bold enough in your faith to simply obey Jesus commission. The signs will follow you.

Mark 16:17

And these signs will follow those who believe: In My name they will cast out demons;…

More On The Devil And Your 'Flesh'

As we have seen, the devil will exploit any 'place' you give him. If you yield your flesh for his purposes, he will corrupt your natural desires and appetites. The flesh is that part of our human makeup that is not spirit. It comprises the unrenewed mind or thought processes, as well as our bodily appetites, passions and drives. Your flesh has to be actively **presented to God** for it to be sanctified. If you do not present your body with its fleshly passions to the Lord, you give satan unnecessary opportunities to influence you.

Romans 12:1

I beseech you therefore, brethren, by the mercies of God, that you present your bodies a living sacrifice, holy, acceptable to God, which is your reasonable service.

What many people often call a direct work of the devil is actually a work of the flesh, or the old, unregenerate part of man's nature that is not yet yielded to God. When the flesh is not under God's control it comes under demonic influence to produce 'fleshly' acts or works.

The 'works of the flesh' are listed below, and include such things as idolatry and witchcraft which are often attributed to demonic activity.

Galatians 5:19-21
Now the works of the flesh are evident, which are: adultery, fornication, uncleanness, lewdness, idolatry, sorcery, hatred, contentions, jealousies, outbursts of wrath, selfish ambitions, dissensions, heresies, envy, murders, drunkenness, revelries, and the like; ...

The Bible teaches that these are works of the flesh and not necessarily an evil spirit. There may be a spirit hiding in the background that influences a person in a certain direction to do evil, but you cannot 'cast out' a demon of jealousy, for example. The person needs to have the truth and security of the gospel take hold of them in this area. Then they will be set free from jealousy. The point here is not to lay the blame on a devil in every instance. The flesh may be involved. You have to discern what is applicable in every case; otherwise, you will be inaccurate and ineffective in dealing with people's problems.

The Bible teaches that the way to deal with these fleshly issues is to 'put off' the old man and 'put on' the new man. That is, you have to make definite choices to obey God's Word. God empowers those that do this with His strength and ability to live a holy life. His grace is what enables you to walk in the freedom that Jesus purchased at Calvary. Grace is God's favor and enabling power to live the life of holiness.

Tiresome spiritual warfare practices are most often 'fleshly' themselves. I have heard of some misguided Christians marching around in combat boots and camouflage gear yelling at the devil. This form of 'spiritual warfare' may be visually dramatic, but it is still unscriptural, and surely leads to a defeated life at best, and oppression and confusion at worst.

Keep your focus on God's beauty, majesty and power. Let these be your magnificent obsession, and do not shift your gaze to the attention grabbing devices of the devil.

Ephesians 4:20-24
But you have not so learned Christ, if indeed you have heard Him and have been taught by Him, as the truth is in Jesus: that you put off, concerning your former conduct, the old man which grows corrupt according

to the deceitful lusts, and be renewed in the spirit of your mind, and that you put on the new man which was created according to God, in true righteousness and holiness.

This passage highlights the definite choice you need to make to forsake the old man, be renewed in the spirit of your mind and the value of identifying with the new man in Christ. Once again, the focus is on God and what he expects us to do, and not on the adversary.

Transformation comes by renewing the mind: where you choose to think new thoughts, speak new words, and do new deeds of mercy and love. When you identify totally with Christ and His ways, there is no place for the devil and his ways.

Learn to 'put on' your new spiritual clothing. Your new robe of righteousness sets you apart. See yourself in right standing with God, and act accordingly. In your prayers and conversation agree with God's view of your new position, and declare that you are the righteousness of God in Christ.

2 Corinthians 5:21
For He made Him who knew no sin to be sin for us, that we might become the righteousness of God in Him.

You render the enemy powerless when you are equipped with the truth about your new creation realities. 'Put on' or identify with all that Jesus has freely given you.

Colossians 3:12-14

Therefore, as the elect of God, holy and beloved, put on tender mercies, kindness, humility, meekness, longsuffering; bearing with one another, and for-giving one another, if anyone has a complaint against another; even as Christ forgave you, so you also must do. But above all these things put on love, which is the bond of perfection.

God expects us to play our part: we must 'put on' tender mercies, kindness, forgiveness and love. When we do, we give no place for the lusts of the flesh. There is no soil for the enemy to sow his seeds of destruction into. Evil does not grow in the soil of love.

We are also taught to 'mortify' or put to death unclean 'members' of our flesh or body through obedience. The fol-lowing scriptures speak of the measures we must take in spiritual warfare.

Colossians 3:5-6

Therefore put to death your members which are on the earth: fornication, uncleanness, passion, evil desire, and covetousness, which is idolatry. Because of these things the wrath of God is coming upon the sons of disobedience, ...

Galatians 5:24-26
And those who are Christ's have crucified the flesh with its passions and desires. If we live in the Spirit, let us also walk in the Spirit.

Even temptation has to do with unsanctified desires of the flesh.

James 1:13-14
Let no one say when he is tempted, "I am tempted by God"; for God cannot be tempted by evil, nor does He Himself tempt anyone. But each one is tempted when he is drawn away by his own desires and enticed.

God expects us to give no place to fleshly lusts. He expects us to yield to Him, and 'possess' or control our own flesh. He will not do it for us, as He knows that we already have the power to do it ourselves.

1 Thessalonians 4:3-5
For this is the will of God, your sanctification: that you should abstain from sexual immorality; that each of you should know how to possess his own vessel in

sanctification and honor, not in passion of lust, like the Gentiles who do not know God;

1 John 4:4

You are of God, little children, and have overcome them, because He who is in you is greater than he who is in the world.

God's will is clear: we have the Holy Spirit to live within and empower us to overcome evil. The key is to present yourself to God or 'yield' to Him. God will not force you to do anything. He leads but does not drive. He wants you make a faith based choice to trust in His abundant and everlasting love.

Romans 6:19

...For just as you presented your members as slaves of uncleanness, and of lawlessness leading to more lawlessness, so now present your members as slaves of righteousness for holiness.

Steps To Walking In Victory

In summary, live out your daily life in the power of the Holy Spirit who lives in you (Galatians 5:16-17). Consecrate to present your body as a living sacrifice (Romans 12:1-2). Fear or reverence God and His favor will surround you as a protective shield (Psalm 115:11). Be alert, watchful and vigilant in prayer for any attack. God reveals anything that is hidden and ready to ensnare you (1 Peter 5:8). Be sure to wear your spiritual armor. Know what belongs to you in the covenant and how to use it (Ephesians 6:10-20). Let your obedience to the Lord disarm and disorientate your enemy.

The following prophecy illustrates the power of consecration. The Lord's consecration is described before it ever happened. He entrusted His life to His heavenly Father before He went to the cross, and was confident that he would not be ashamed in the conflict.

Isaiah 50:5-7
The Lord GOD has opened My ear;
And I was not rebellious,
Nor did I turn away.
I gave My back to those who struck Me,
And My cheeks to those who plucked out the beard;
I did not hide My face from shame and spitting.
"For the Lord GOD will help Me;
Therefore I will not be disgraced;
Therefore I have set My face like a flint,
And I know that I will not be ashamed.

When you know the Father's loving nature; who you are in Christ, and that your adversary is defeated, then spiritual warfare takes on a whole new light, and is marked by a confidence that the enemy is already defeated before any engagement.

Devil And Demons Summary Fact Sheet

• Devil Definition: accuser / tempter / adversary.
Revelation 12:10 / Matthew 4:1 / 1 Peter 5:8

• Created perfect as an angel: 'Lucifer' or light bearer.
Isaiah 14:12-15 / Ezekiel 28:11-17

• Fell due to pride, and renamed satan.
Revelation 12:9

• Corrupted mankind in the Garden of Eden.
Genesis 3:1-11

• Can transform into an 'angel of light' to deceive.
2 Corinthians 11:14

• Uses demons of varying wickedness and rank under his control to 'distribute' evil.
Matthew 12:45 / Ephesians 6:12 /Matthew 9:34

• Demons can oppress, intimidate and possess unsuspecting people.
Acts 10:38 / 2 Timothy 1:7 / Acts 16:16

• Satan and demons exploit human ignorance, and disobedience.
Hosea 4:6 / 2 Corinthians 2:11 /Ephesians 2:2

• Defeated and disarmed by the Lord Jesus Christ.
Colossians 2:15-16

• Any Christian has authority over satan and any demon.
Luke 10:17-20 / Mark 16:15-20

• Must be actively resisted by the believer.
Matthew 4:4 / Ephesians 6:13 / James 4:7

• Demonic activity should not be confused with 'works' of the flesh.
Galatians 5:19-21

It is our privilege to 'pierce the darkness' with light, obedience and hope. Intercessory prayer is part of this process.

Chapter 7

Your Authority In Prayer

จฺ ๑๏

Prayer Is A Powerful Tool In Spiritual Warfare

Prayer is the process by which you get your needs met and how God's will is established on earth as it is in heaven. Through covenant based prayer, you partner with God to enforce satan's defeat on the earth. Prayer lays the foundation for any effective ministry, and is not some religious activity to keep you busy and God satisfied. It is a powerful tool in spiritual warfare that is highly effective in thwarting satan's plans.

James 5:16
...The effective, fervent prayer of a righteous man avails much.

Prayer is always directed with one of three focuses: on God in praise, our need in petition, or in intercession on behalf of others in their need. This chapter concentrates on intercession and our prayer authority.

Who Should Pray And Intercede?

Ezekiel 22:30

So I sought for a man among them who would make a wall, and stand in the gap before Me on behalf of the land, …

1 Thessalonians 5:25

Brethren, pray for us.

All Christians are called not only to pray for their own needs, but also intercede for others in their need. Intercession simply means to 'plead' on behalf of someone else. God is looking for anyone who will 'stand in the gap' that has opened up to the enemy in someone's life. When you intercede for someone you effectively 'stand in the gap' for them and invoke God's protection and provision on their behalf. Intercessors are those that respond to His call to pray for others on a regular basis. As an example, Anna the prophetess spent her nights and days in fasting and prayer. She was an intercessor whose primary role, it appears, was to lay a prayer foundation for the first coming of Christ.

Luke 2:36-38 36

Now there was one, Anna, a prophetess, the daughter of Phanuel, of the tribe of Asher. She was of a great age, and had lived with a husband seven years from her virginity; 37 and this woman was a widow of about eighty-four years, who did not depart from the temple, but served God with fastings and prayers night and day. 38 And coming in that instant she gave thanks to the Lord, and spoke of Him to all those who looked for redemption in Jerusalem.

Scripture does not teach that intercession is the special domain of some specially gifted people, but rather that intercession should be part of every Christian's prayer life. I believe as Christians grow in their walk with the Lord, they take on an increasing burden to pray, not only for their own needs, but for the needs of others. As a Christian matures their prayer life becomes less selfish and more selfless. God has called all believers to proclaim the good news to the whole world that lies in the darkness of ignorance, disobedience and despair (Mark 16:15). It is our privilege to 'pierce the darkness' with light, obedience and hope. Intercessory prayer is part of this process. It is vital to pray for our brothers and sisters in Christ so that we all enjoy the enlightenment and strength needed to continue doing what God has called us to do.

There are two key prayers the apostle Paul prayed in the book of Ephesians that teach us how to pray for each other in the areas of spiritual enlightenment and strength. First, consider the 'prayer of enlightenment'.

The Prayer Of Enlightenment

Ephesians 1:15-19

Therefore I also, after I heard of your faith in the Lord Jesus and your love for all the saints, do not cease to give thanks for you, making mention of you in my prayers: that the God of our Lord Jesus Christ, the Father of glory, may give to you the spirit of wisdom and revelation in the knowledge of Him, the eyes of your understanding being enlightened; that you may know what is the hope of His calling, what are the riches of the glory of His inheritance in the saints, and what is the exceeding greatness of His power toward us who believe,...

When Christians walk in the light, and it is not automatic that they always do, their witness is effective. People still in spiritual darkness and sin are attracted to the 'light' that now shines in the believer's life. If, on the other hand, Christians do not walk in the light, their influence is limited, and their witness compromised. They are not functioning as light in the world. To walk in the light, you have to have your eyes opened to the hope of your calling. This is the stuff of spiritual warfare and prayer. God has already paid the price for our spiritual victory. He has won the battle in Christ.

A key in spiritual warfare is for believers to see things from His perspective: to see what is actually going on in a situation. We must have God's light or perspective ('enlightened') to be effective. That is why Paul made it his business as an intercessor to pray this prayer over the saints.

Again, in an Old Testament example, Elisha had to pray for his servant to see into the spirit realm. His servant was overwhelmed by what appeared to be a hopeless battle situation. At this point he could only see with his 'natural' eye, and things looked serious. So Elisha prayed for his 'enlightenment'.

2 Kings 6:15-17

And when the servant of the man of God arose early and went out, there was an army, surrounding the city with horses and chariots. And his servant said to him, "Alas, my master! What shall we do?" So he answered, "Do not fear, for those who are with us are more than those who are with them." And Elisha prayed, and said, "LORD, I pray, open his eyes that he may see." Then the LORD opened the eyes of the young man, and he saw. And behold, the mountain was full of horses and chariots of fire all around Elisha.

The forces of the Lord were always there, but God opened the servant's spiritual eyes to a higher reality or truth, and as a consequence his faith arose.

However, once a believer is enlightened to their calling, they still face spiritual opposition from the adversary. In order to stay strong in the Lord and stand their ground, 'strengthening' prayer is also needed.

The Prayer For Strengthening

Ephesians 3:14-16

For this reason I bow my knees to the Father of our Lord Jesus Christ, from whom the whole family in heaven and earth is named, that He would grant you, according to the riches of His glory, to be strengthened with might through His Spirit in the inner man, ...

When Christians remain strong in the faith, their witness in the community is effective, and the gospel advances. However, when they are weak and timid, their witness is watered down, and satan's hold on the lost is largely unaffected. Intercessory prayer for other believers to be and stay strong in the Lord is also the stuff of spiritual warfare.

Make it your practice to pray regularly for yourself and fellow believers (especially your leaders) to be enlightened and filled with strength according to the above two prayers in Ephesians. Personalize the prayers by putting your own name, that of your leaders and even fellow believers you know.

Praying 'Against' The Devil and Demons Is Not Scriptural

Neither Jesus nor the apostles prayed 'against' satan and evil spirits. They always directed their prayers and intercessions to God the Father for their own spiritual well-being and alertness. When Jesus was faced with intense spiritual pressure in the Garden of Gethsemane, He spoke of praying to be spiritually alert and vigilant, and not about 'binding' some evil, religious spirit in Jerusalem at the time!

Matthew 26:41
Watch and pray, lest you enter into temptation. The spirit indeed is willing, but the flesh is weak."

Jesus also prayed for unity among believers (John 17), and that Peter's faith would not fail (Luke 22:31-32). The focus was always on standing strong in their relationships with God and with one another. When these relationships are vibrant and real, the adversary has no place to move, and the gospel advances more readily. Intercession keeps the focus on what God is doing, and not on what the adversary is up to. Do not make his deeds the focus of you attention. Keep God and His praise central to your prayer life.

How To Pray For The Lost

There are several key prayer pointers here.

First, pray to the Lord of the Harvest to 'thrust' out laborers into the harvest field of souls. This prayer is part of spiritual warfare.

Matthew 9:36-38

But when He saw the multitudes, He was moved with compassion for them, because they were weary and scattered, like sheep having no shepherd. Then He said to His disciples, "The harvest truly is plentiful, but the laborers are few. Therefore pray the Lord of the harvest to send out laborers into His harvest."

When Jesus saw the need in His own ministry even, He solicited the help of His disciples to pray for more gospel workers. This ought to be a vital part of praying for the lost.

Second, as believers we are to prepare the soil of the unbeliever's heart so that when the gospel is preached to them they are receptive to it. This involves 'travail' or 'intense labor' as is common in natural childbirth. Prayer travail must be 'in the spirit', with the help of the Holy Spirit who prays through us. He helps us pray effectively in situations where we do not know exactly how to pray. Paul described prayer travail in these terms.

Galatians 4:19

My little children, for whom I labor in birth again until Christ is formed in you,

He had previously labored as 'in birth' for them to get born again in the first place, and now he was laboring in travailing prayer **again** that they would have Christ formed in them. The focus was now that they would grow up in their relationship with Christ. In both instances prayer labor or travail was needed: first to get born again into God's family, and then to grow up in God's family!

When the proclaimed Word gains entrance into the unbeliever, spiritual light comes, and a decision for Christ can be made. This convicting work of the Holy Spirit is a direct consequence of preaching the Word and prayer for receptive hearts. The Word has to penetrate or gain entrance past barriers of doubt and unbelief.

Psalm 119:130

The entrance of Your words gives light; It gives understanding to the simple.

Faith for salvation arises in the hearts of unbelievers when the soil of their hearts is prepared, and the gospel is preached to them.

Romans 10:17-18

So then faith comes by hearing, and hearing by the word of God.

Third, pray for the 'laborers in the harvest' to enjoy protection and deliverance from wicked and unreasonable men (2 Thessalonians 3:1-2). I know of a preacher in my native South Africa who was distracted off his calling and life's purpose by a wicked and unreasonable man. His ministry was lost as well as his marriage. Pray for your leaders. This is all part of spiritual warfare and reaching the lost.

Fourth, pray that doors of opportunity open up to fellow believers to share the gospel.

Colossians 4:2-3

Continue earnestly in prayer, being vigilant in it with thanksgiving; meanwhile praying also for us, that God would open to us a door for the word, to speak the mystery of Christ, ...

Fifth, pray for continued boldness to speak God's Word in the face of intimidation. The enemy knows the power that there is in the Word, so he instigates persecution in an attempt to stop the Word from being boldly proclaimed. As we have seen the early church was threatened by the religious authorities not to preach the word, so they got together and prayed to the Lord. Notice, they did not get sidetracked into some unorthodox manner of spiritual warfare. They simply kept their focus on God and the commission He gave to them. Their prayer request focused on God granting them boldness to continue what He had already commissioned them to do.

A sixth scriptural way to engage in spiritual warfare is to pray for those in authority in your sphere of influence. The apostle Paul said that we are to make this a priority, because when there is godliness in government, it has a positive bearing on peace and the freedom needed for the gospel to go out unhindered by war and strife. A war torn, or strife filled community is a difficult environment for a strong gospel witness. Modern history has testified to this in nations like Rwanda and the Sudan where war and ongoing strife has hindered the gospel.

1 Timothy 2:1-4
Therefore I exhort first of all that supplications, prayers, intercessions, and giving of thanks be made for all men, for kings and all who are in authority, that we may lead a quiet and peaceable life in all godliness and reverence. For this is good and acceptable in the sight of God our Savior, who desires all men to be saved and to come to the knowledge of the truth.

Here is a sample prayer to pray when praying specifically for the lost. Mention specific people by name as you pray.

"Father God, I bring _____ before You. I know with confidence that it is Your will for them to be saved and come to the knowledge of Your truth in Jesus. Give me and other laborers the boldness, wisdom and opportunity to witness effectively to them. Soften their hearts Lord God by Your gracious Holy Spirit. I declare that satan is bound from lying to them. May Your word pierce their hearts and 'gain entrance' so that they may repent and accept Jesus as Savior and Lord. I praise and thank you for their salvation. In Jesus' name, Amen."

How To Pray For Your Nation

In God's eyes, the nations belong to Him. He has chosen and called the church in any nation to be the preserving 'salt and light'. The welfare of a whole nation is thus dependent on the degree to which the church in that nation is functioning as salt and light. Have you ever heard of groups of ungodly unbelievers getting together to beseech the Lord for the welfare of the nation. Of course not! It is up to believers to pray and bring change to their nation.

2 Chronicles 7:14-15
"If My people who are called by My name will humble themselves, and pray and seek My face, and turn from their wicked ways, then I will hear from heaven, and will forgive their sin and heal their land.

Now My eyes will be open and My ears attentive to prayer made in this place."

Holiness is not reserved for super saints but is God's calling on all Christians. When God's people live holy lives, they walk in more authority than when they are ignorant of their righteousness in Christ. Sin, whether in private or public, has a weakening effect. In our New Testament context we are already forgiven in Christ, and God is attentive to our prayers not because of our personal efforts to be holy, but rather because Jesus is holy, and we are in Him!

When we truly see God's goodness extended to us in Christ, we change and forsake wicked ways (repent according to Romans 2:4). Also, when we realize that we are holy because of Christ's finished work, we step up and fulfill our call to live right, and our prayers are effective.

James 5:16
The effective, fervent prayer of a righteous man avails much.

Pray For Your Nation Using These Pointers

Pray …

• That righteousness will prevail in the nation and evil will be exposed. Proverbs 14:34 / Ephesians 5:11

• That God will supernaturally intervene and favor His righteous cause. Psalm 35:27

• That God will extend mercy and not judgment on the nation. James 2:13

• That God-fearing men and women who do not show partiality nor take bribes or twist words will be promoted to office. Deuteronomy 16:19 / Psalm 75:6-7

• That those in authority will restrain evil, promote good and govern with justice in the fear of God. Romans 13:1- 4

• That the unborn, the aged, the innocent, and the poor will be protected. Jeremiah 2:34

• That all believers might have peace and freedom to preach the gospel in the nation. 2 Thessalonians 3:1

Pointed and scriptural prayer is one of the most powerful weapons in spiritual warfare. Earth's need connects with Heaven's provision when effectual fervent prayer is offered to God in faith. This is the stuff of spiritual warfare.

Prayer Of Protection Psalm 91

You are on a mission to fulfill God's plans and purposes for your life. Satan's goal is to steal, kill and destroy; so as part of your defense, pray this prayer out loud each day, personalizing the scripture. As you meet the conditions, you can claim in faith the promises of protection that God has made in this scripture. The parts that are in italics are the parts of the original psalm that are personalized for your use.

Declaration of the Lord's promised protection

1 (I) dwell in the secret place of the Most High (and) abide under the shadow of the Almighty. 2 (I) say of the LORD, "(You are) my refuge and my fortress; my God, in You do (I) trust."

3 Surely (You) deliver (me) from the snare of the fowler and from the perilous pestilence. 4 (You) cover (me) with (Your) feathers, and under (Your) wings (I) take refuge; (Your) truth (is my) shield and buckler. 5 (I am) not afraid of the terror by night, nor of the arrow that flies by day, 6 Nor of the pestilence that walks in darkness, nor of the destruction that lays waste at noonday. 7 A thousand may fall at (my) side, and ten thousand at (my) right hand; but it shall not come near (me). 8 Only with (my) eyes shall (I) look, and see the reward of the wicked. 9 Because (I) have made the LORD, my refuge, even the Most High, (my) dwelling place, 10 No evil shall befall (me), nor shall any plague come near (my) dwelling; 11 For He

shall give His angels charge over (me), to keep (me) in all (my) ways. 12 In their hands they shall bear (me) up, lest (I) dash (my) foot against a stone. 13 (I) shall tread upon the lion and the cobra, the young lion and the serpent (I) shall trample underfoot.

The Lord's Response

14 "Because (you have) set (your) love upon Me, therefore I will deliver (you); I will set (you) on high, because (you) has known My name. 15 (You) shall call upon Me, and I will answer (you); I will be with (you) in trouble; I will deliver (you) and honor (you). 16 With long life I will satisfy (you), and show (you) My salvation." Believe and expect God to honor His Word in your life and protect you and your family as you faithfully serve Him.

It is vital that the church realize that worship is not merely some prelude to Sunday morning preaching, but a vital lifestyle of adoration that is powerfully linked to God's plan for man.

Chapter 8

Authority And The Power Of Worship

୶ଚ ଚ୬

God Is A Musical God

Music and song is referenced over eight hundred times in the Bible. Throughout history armies have marched to the sound of music. The importance of music and song cannot be overemphasized in both the private and corporate life of every believer. God is a musical God, and the inventor of all that is good in this field of human expression. The Bible teaches that He even sings over us with great joy.

Zephaniah 3:17
The LORD your God in your midst, The Mighty One, will save; He will rejoice over you with gladness, He

will quiet you with His love, He will rejoice over you with singing."

All singers get their talent from the greatest singer of them all: God. Thank God for those who have consecrated their gift of music and song to bring Him glory. I believe that when we hear inspired music and song, we hear the voice of the Lord singing through them. On earth, God uses the instrumentality of man to rejoice over us. We continue this stream of rejoicing when make melody in our hearts by the power of His Spirit.

Ephesians 5:18-19
...be filled with the Spirit, speaking to one another in psalms and hymns and spiritual songs, singing and making melody in your heart to the Lord, ...

When we speak, sing and minister to one another we do so on God's behalf.

Worship And Warfare

God created Lucifer as one of His covering cherub angels, and anointed him to lead worship in heaven. He was anointed to give worship to God but not to receive it for himself. Worship is reserved for God alone. It appears that musical instruments may even have been built into his very being.

Ezekiel 28:12-15

...You were the seal of perfection, Full of wisdom and perfect in beauty. You were in Eden, the garden of God; Every precious stone was your covering: The sardius, topaz, and diamond, Beryl, onyx, and jasper, Sapphire, turquoise, and emerald with gold. The workmanship of your timbrels and pipes Was prepared for you on the day you were created.

Tabrets speak of percussion instruments, pipes of wind instruments, and viols of stringed instruments. These constitute the three main categories of all musical instruments today. Yet a time came when iniquity was found in Lucifer. He was created perfect and thus all evil originated from him and not from God as we saw earlier on in Chapter Six. The first sin of pride and rebellion was thus in heaven and not on earth! This rebellion was carried to earth when Adam was tempted in the garden by satan (the fallen Lucifer now cast out of heaven). Satan's independent will, rebellion and self exaltation led to his downfall. God could not tolerate this impurity in His midst and was obliged to cast him out of heaven.

Adam had authority on earth over every creeping thing, so it was not unfair to him to experience the temptation of satan, the serpent or poisoner. Adam could have (and should have) run satan off, but he did not hearken to God's clear command given earlier to him in the garden. When Adam yielded to the temptation, he became corrupted, and his nature changed. He now had a fallen nature. Sadly, the motivation of all music was also corrupted by sin, and throughout the ages mankind has not always glorified God with his music and song. In fact, the devil has used the power of music and song to captivate whole generations.

Thankfully, today there are an increasing number of musicians and singers sold out to God who are impacting the world for Him through their anointed music. Modern means of communication have rapidly spread their influence around the world, and millions have been uplifted and energized in a godly way by their music.

Satan experienced and recognized the power resident in heavenly worship before he fell, and he has always craved the worship due to God. So when Jesus (God in the flesh), was manifest on the earth, satan sought to tempt Jesus to bow to him in worship. He knew that if Jesus could be corrupted in His worship, He (Jesus) would come under his (satan's) control. Worship and lordship (and thus authority in the spirit realm) are interconnected.

Matthew 4:8-10

Again, the devil took Him up on an exceedingly high mountain, and showed Him all the kingdoms of the world and their glory. And he said to Him, "All these things I will give You if You will fall down and worship me." Then Jesus said to him, "Away with you,

Satan! For it is written, 'You shall worship the LORD your God, and Him only you shall serve.'"

It is vital that the church realize that worship is not merely some prelude to Sunday morning preaching, but a vital lifestyle of adoration that is powerfully linked to God's plan for man. In fact, God expects all worship to be offered in 'spirit and truth' and for our private and public worship to reflect His glory at all times. However many believers restrict their worship in time and space to a particular church building on a particular day!

John 4:23-24

"But the hour is coming, and now is, when the true worshipers will worship the Father in spirit and truth; for the Father is seeking such to worship Him. God is Spirit, and those who worship Him must worship in spirit and truth."

God is looking for a lifestyle of worship where all that we are, say and do is our worship to Him! We actually become 'instruments' of worship in His hands. He wants the world to hear the music of our lives as a witness to them.

Examples Of Worship And Warfare

There are many instances of God's people engaging in praise and worship that served as a weapon in the spiritual fight they faced. In the following example, God's people, under Joshua's leadership, were to take the city of Jericho as they crossed over the Jordan River and enter their Promised Land. They were on the offensive but not in their own strength or power. They were to take the city with 'effortless' yet supernatural force.

Joshua 6:1-5

Now Jericho was securely shut up because of the children of Israel; none went out, and none came in. And the LORD said to Joshua: "See! I have given Jericho into your hand, its king, and the mighty men of valor. You shall march around the city, all you men of war; you shall go all around the city once. This you shall do six days. And seven priests shall bear seven trumpets of rams' horns before the ark. But the seventh day you shall march around the city seven times, and the priests shall blow the trumpets. It shall come to pass, when they make a long blast with the ram's horn, and when you hear the sound of the trumpet, that all the people shall shout with a great shout; then the wall of the city will fall down flat. And the people shall go up every man straight before him."

They had specific instructions that made no sense to them in the natural. Archaeologists report that the walls of

Jericho were hugely thick and strong, big enough to even build houses on top of them. Yet the Bible records that these strong walls would fall down flat at the sound of a long trumpet blast and a shout from all the people of God! The trumpets speak of music and the shout of the people speaks of praise. Here warfare was to be effected though music and praise! It seems clear that God was giving His people a strong object lesson in this first step of possessing their Promised Land. He wanted them to preface everything they did with praise and worship. The supernatural sound went out, and the walls came down just as God had promised! The faith and obedience of the priests and the people paved the way for supernatural victory. Their obedience, together with praise and worship, defeated the enemy.

A second example of worship and warfare is found in the story of King Jehoshaphat where he and the people of Israel were on the defensive. The armies of Moab and Ammon came up in vast numbers against the Israelites who became fearful, yet sought the Lord through prayer and fasting under Jehoshaphat's leadership. The Spirit of the Lord came upon one of the Levites who prophesied to the assembly that the battle would be the Lord's and not theirs. Details are given of where, when and how they were to 'engage' with the enemy. They responded to the promise of deliverance with thankful praise and worship to the Lord. They went out the next morning on the day of the battle, and King Jehoshaphat addressed his people with these words:

2 Chronicles 20:20-22

..."Hear me, O Judah and you inhabitants of Jerusalem: Believe in the LORD your God, and you shall be established; believe His prophets, and you shall prosper." And when he had consulted with the people, he appointed those who should sing to the LORD, and who should praise the beauty of holiness, as they went out before the army and were saying: "Praise the LORD, For His mercy endures forever." Now when they began to sing and to praise, the LORD set ambushes against the people of Ammon, Moab, and Mount Seir, who had come against Judah; and they were defeated.

A mighty victory was won that day through faith, obedience and the presence of the Lord invoked through praise and worship. Ambushes were set by the Lord and the enemy was defeated.

Wherever God's people praise the Lord, His presence is experienced, and the enemy cannot remain long in God's presence. That is why demon manifestations often occur during praise and worship sessions. They react to God's holiness. The awesome power of praise and worship cannot be over estimated. The Israelites returned to Jerusalem with the abundant spoils of war and continued to rejoice for the Lord's supernatural intervention.

It is always beneficial to engage in praise and worship when faced with an aggressor. When you commit to release your faith in praise, the enemy is 'ambushed' and this form of spiritual warfare produces thrilling victories.

A Key To The Kingdom

Two Psalms reveal a fascinating revelation of the authority we wield as the 'saints' of God. The foundation is laid in Psalm Two, where the ungodly attitude of the nations and its peoples towards the restraining influences of the Lord is revealed. They vainly seek to be free from the 'bonds' and the 'cords' that hold back their evil. When you look at the world today, there are rulers and nations that set themselves against God, the Lord Jesus Christ and His purposes. They do so by opposing God's church in some way or another.

Psalm 2:1-3

Why do the nations rage, And the people plot a vain thing? The kings of the earth set themselves, And the rulers take counsel together, Against the LORD and against His Anointed, saying, "Let us break their bonds in pieces And cast away their cords from us."

Psalm 149 speaks of the authority and honor that saints have in the field of praise and worship. This has everything to do with spiritual warfare! Their joyful song of praise executes 'vengeance' on the nations and 'binds' their kings with chains. Their nobles are also restrained with fetters of iron. This speaks of the powerful and significant consequence of a lifestyle of praise and worship!

> Psalm 149:5-9
>
> Let the saints be joyful in glory; Let them sing aloud on their beds. Let the high praises of God be in their mouth, And a two-edged sword in their hand, To execute vengeance on the nations, And punishments on the peoples; To bind their kings with chains, And their nobles with fetters of iron; To execute on them the written judgment— This honor have all His saints. Praise the LORD!

In the same way that satanic music and song looses demonic influence in people, Godly music and song **binds** the work of the enemy! Praise and worship, alongside prayer and the preaching of God's Word (the 'two-edged sword) is central in spiritual warfare. When believers are weak in their praise, the enemy is more at liberty to move in their lives. But when the high praises of God resound with great rejoicing, the enemy is bound!

I believe this is one of the keys of the kingdom that Jesus spoke of to Peter when God had shown him Jesus' true identity. When we get a revelation of Jesus true identity and nature, our praises will also bind the enemy. Make it your practice to fill your dwelling with praise music and song. Sing praises to God as you go about your daily doings at home and even at work where you can. You invoke God's presence as you do, and run off the enemy too.

Matthew 16:16-19

Simon Peter answered and said, "You are the Christ, the Son of the living God." Jesus answered and said to him, "Blessed are you, Simon Bar-Jonah, for flesh and blood has not revealed this to you, but My Father who is in heaven. And I also say to you that you are Peter, and on this rock I will build My church, and the gates of Hades shall not prevail against it. And I will give you the keys of the kingdom of heaven, and whatever you bind on earth will be bound in heaven, and whatever you loose on earth will be loosed in heaven."

Keys speak of authority, and when you praise God you exercise authority over evil.

The Worship Anointing

Where God's presence is manifest, His power is also demonstrated. Jesus was teaching one day in a house and the power of God was present to heal all those present with Him. Because of their ungodly mental reasoning, unbelief and skepticism of the Pharisees and teachers of the law from Jerusalem, not one of them got healed.

> Luke 5:17-17
> Now it happened on a certain day, as He was teaching, that there were Pharisees and teachers of the law sitting by, who had come out of every town of Galilee, Judea, and Jerusalem. And the power of the Lord was present to heal them.

Only when the paralytic was brought by his friends in faith to be healed did the healing anointing or power flow out of Jesus to affect his miracle cure. The healed man rose to his feet and glorified God along with others in the house.

> Luke 5:24-26
> …He said to the man who was paralyzed, "I say to you, arise, take up your bed, and go to your house." Immediately he rose up before them, took up what he had been lying on, and departed to his own house, glorifying God. And they were all amazed, and they glorified God …

In this account we see the works of the evil one destroyed through a combination of faith, healing anointing and worship. On another occasion, a leper approached Jesus and worshiped Him. He wanted to be clean, and Jesus showed both His willingness and ability to heal this leprous man by stretching out His hand and touching him.

Matthew 8:1-3
When He had come down from the mountain, great multitudes followed Him. And behold, a leper came and worshiped Him, saying, "Lord, if You are willing, You can make me clean." Then Jesus put out His hand and touched him, saying, "I am willing; be cleansed." Immediately his leprosy was cleansed.

The Word even teaches that God is favorably disposed to grant worshipers what they need. In other words, He hears worshippers!

John 9:31
Now we know that God does not hear sinners; but if anyone is a worshiper of God and does His will, He hears him.

Still in the arena of spiritual warfare against sickness and disease, we see in the following scripture the vital importance of being joyful or merry.

Proverbs 17:22
A merry heart does good, like medicine, But a broken spirit dries the bones.

Spiritual warfare involves a straightforward walk with the Lord in obedience to His ways. A lifestyle of worship is one of His ways.

Ephesians 5:18-21
And do not be drunk with wine, in which is dissipation; but be filled with the Spirit, speaking to one another in psalms and hymns and spiritual songs, singing and making melody in your heart to the Lord, giving thanks always for all things to God the Father in the name of our Lord Jesus Christ, submitting to one another in the fear of God.

The Spirit-filled life involves a continuing joyful and thankful celebration of God's goodness through music and song. When you establish a lifestyle of praise and worship, the enemy is left out in the cold. He craves attention, and should not be given any, except to cast him out where necessary.

In the following passage we see an example of how worship warfare is waged in the arena of prayer. Anxiety is a form of fear that is unsettling, destroys peace, and attacks our hearts and minds. When we chose to obey God in faith, give thanks to Him, and pray our requests and not our problems, our hearts and minds are 'guarded' against the enemy onslaughts.

Philippians 4:6-7

Be anxious for nothing, but in everything by prayer and supplication, with thanksgiving, let your requests be made known to God; and the peace of God, which surpasses all understanding, will guard your hearts and minds through Christ Jesus. Thankfulness towards God is like a shield of protection in the fight of faith. Thankfulness also protects our inner man from becoming hardened.

What Happens When We Mix Prayer With Praise And Worship?

Deliverance from desperate situations comes through mixing prayer with praise and worship. Paul and Silas had been faithfully serving God and suffered intense persecution for their obedience. The enemy was stirred up, and moved the citizens of the city of Ephesus to bring false charges against their ministry. The magistrates of the city threw them in prison after having had them unjustly beaten with rods. At midnight, Paul and Silas were still awake and faced with a choice: complain or consider God's goodness! They decided to pray and praise God. Perhaps it took them hours to recover enough strength to lift up their voices loud enough for the other prisoners to hear them.

Acts 16:25-26

But at midnight Paul and Silas were praying and singing hymns to God, and the prisoners were listening to them. Suddenly there was a great earthquake, so that the foundations of the prison were shaken; and immediately all the doors were opened and everyone's chains were loosed.

Their deliverance from their seemingly hopeless situation was dramatic enough. Their prayer mixed with worship moved heaven, and the earth shook with an earthquake that loosened not only their chains, but that of everyone else too. God then used the freed Apostles to minister to the distraught prison keeper and his whole family, who promptly got saved. Paul and Silas refused to flee, and later enjoyed considerable favor with the magistrates who had earlier thrown them in prison. Now afraid, the magistrates formally brought them out into the community, and let them go. Never underestimate what God will do for you in a tight spot as you mix your praise with your prayers.

A Word Of Balance

God has commissioned the church to reach the world in His name. The church must at the same time cultivate a lifestyle of true worship in spirit and truth. This field of ministry should never be neglected.

However, prayer, praise and worship ought never to become a cozy substitute for reaching out to the lost and needy as we are commanded to do. Some churches 'camp around the throne' and seem never to come down off the mountain top heights of experiencing the presence of God. They love praise and worship services, but do little in reaching the lost. After every time Jesus withdrew to be alone with His Father in heaven, He always came back to meet the needs of the people He was called to seek, serve and save. When we worship it is like breathing in His power. But after 'breathing in', we are expected to 'breathe out' His blessing on others. We are blessed in order to be a blessing!

Truth always dispels error as light always drives out darkness. Faith overcomes fear, and hope and love prevail.

Chapter 9

Authority In The Spirit Realm

In conclusion, one cannot afford to be passive about the spirit realm. Authority that is not exercised is lost or wasted. God is waiting upon the church to step up into its place in His kingdom and exercise its full authority under His Lordship. If we are to reach the whole world with God's goodness we must proclaim the whole gospel with all its supernatural power. 'Normal' Christianity must be replaced with the full force of God's supernatural kingdom presence.

God has promised to build His glorious church, and the gates of hell cannot stand against a triumphant army of believers marching in their God given authority, supported by His angelic hosts, enforcing satan's defeat wherever they go. Demons are no match for the Spirit – filled saint whose eyes have been opened to the authority and power they have in Christ. Seated at His right hand in the heavenlies, they know that to strive against an already defeated foe is only foolishness. Worshipping prayer warriors have the privilege of seeing God do His mighty wonders amongst men, and the enemy's shackles shaken loose to the glory of God.

Truth always dispels error as light always drives out darkness. Fear is overcome by love, and faith hope and love always prevails. God is all powerful, and when you awaken to the authority you have in Christ, your adversary is exposed for the fraud he is. The greater one lives in you.

Put on (make the choice to operate in) your armor of authority, and boldly tread on the 'serpents and scorpions' of the devil as you walk in love, faith and obedience. Use the sword of the spirit (the Word of God that you speak in faith) as your offensive weapon of choice.

Fan the flame of your passion as you are fully convinced of God's purpose for you in His overcoming church. Stand your ground when challenged by the liar, and make it your business to hear the Good Shepherd's voice leading you to places of peace in the midst of turmoil. Expect His angelic support in what you do, and glorify God by stepping up into a new realm of strength and fruitfulness as you help advance His kingdom on earth.

There is a world to reach for Jesus and He wants you to step up into your God delegated authority. Be bold, and be strong, for God is with you. He is greater than anything you will ever face.

If You Have Never Accepted Jesus As Your Lord

God has made it possible for you to get into right relationship with Him.

He sent His Son Jesus into the world to live, die and rise again from the dead so that you could be forgiven of your sins, live a life that pleases Him, and joined to Him forever in heaven when you die.

God expects you to acknowledge your need for His forgiveness, believe that He raised Jesus from the dead, and be prepared to confess Jesus as Lord before witnesses in the world you live in.

Accept His free gift of eternal life today. Turn away from your sinful past, wholeheartedly put your trust in Him today. Pray this prayer out loud from your heart, you will be giving your life back to him, and He will love, protect and provide for you all the days of your life.

Dear God in heaven,
I accept that I need your forgiveness for my sin.
I repent and acknowledge that I cannot save myself.
I believe that you raised your only begotten son Jesus from the dead.
I ask you to come into my heart right now and be my Lord.
I confess you Jesus as the Lord (master) of my life.
I promise to serve you all my days.

Thank you for saving me. I am now your child, accepted into your family.

In Jesus name I pray, Amen.

Signed: _____

Date: _____

Friend,

Now that you have prayed this prayer, get into a trustworthy Bible believing church that focuses on Jesus and His word, read your Bible starting with the gospel of John in the New Testament, and tell someone that you have accepted Jesus as Your Lord. Pray to your new heavenly Father every day, and look to God to help you in every area of your life.

God bless you.

Other Titles By Ed Horak

THE SOUND OF HIS VOICE
God still speaks today! Learn how you can be led by the Holy Spirit and hear the sound of His voice in your everyday life.

VICTIM TO VICTOR
Take practical steps to overcome any "victim mentality" tendencies in your life, and live a victorious life.

HOW TO WALK FREE
Being set free is one thing. Learn the practical steps that are needed to walk in that freedom on a daily basis.

EXCELLENCE OF MINISTRY
A useful reference for all levels of leadership. Ed Horak shares insights from over 25 years of ministry.

WHAT'S NEXT
First steps on your new spiritual journey as a new believer.

THE BELIEVERS BACK PACK SERIES (7 Booklets)
…what you need to know about foundational truths.
FAITH / WORSHIP / PROSPERITY / HEALING / PRAYER / HOLY SPIRIT / WORD

WHAT DOES YOUR FUTURE HOLD?

The future is predictable when you put it in God's hands.

Visit

www.edhorak.com

Breinigsville, PA USA
28 April 2010
236943BV00001B/2/P